Bristol Radical Pam|

Lady Blacks....

The Perils of Perception – suffragettes who became fascists

Rosemary L Caldicott

Copyright © 2017 Rosemary L Caldicott

ISBN 978-1-911522-39-3

Bristol Radical History Group. 2017.

www.brh.org.uk

brh@brh.org.uk

Contents

Acknowledgements

I would like to express my thanks to those who have helped me finish this book. I am extremely grateful for the support and suggestions offered by Dr Roger Ball who proofread my draft. Also, to Richard Musgrove for undertaking a final and comprehensive proofread. It was very kind of Di Parkin, historian, to allow me to include her disclosure of her meeting with Lady Diana Mosley during the 1980s and for reviewing my final draft. Also, I am very appreciative to my colleague John Stevens, political historian, for taking the time to review and offer comment on some of the personalities and politicians I have mentioned, although I am accountable for the views expressed in the book. To Mr Ray Webber, poet, I am very thankful to him for allowing me to interview him and recount his recollections of fascist meetings in Bristol during the 1930s.

Foreword

Why would the 1930s political movement known as the British Union of Fascists appeal to women? And, more significantly to a small group of ultra-nationalistic women who were feminists and former members of the militant suffragette movement – the celebrated Women's Social and Political Union (WSPU)? These were, after all, women who had fought, were imprisoned and tortured so that women could attain the vote. They were undoubtedly politically minded women who enjoyed engagement in radical politics, and for this reason the British Union of Fascists opened over 50 regional branches across England to be known as the Women's Sections, including branches in the South West of England.

This work is an attempt to illuminate the political and social tensions that still confronted women in 1930s Britain, a country that was politically polarised during the inter-war years. What were the issues that were so profound that some women would be steered towards anti-feminist fascism; to become a 'militant woman citizen' – to advocate and endorse fascism?[1]

> The formation of the women's section has filled a great need and is shown by the extraordinary way in which it has grown during the past year. In March 1933 we numbered 17. To-day throughout the country there are women's sections working side by side with the men's branches, and having their own general headquarters at 12, Lower Grosvenor Place [London] …For without a sound knowledge of fascism it is impossible for the women to undertake what is essentially their work for the Movement – that of canvassing!...Another aspect of women's work is the 'Propaganda Patrol' (i.e. selling literature and training in ju-jitsu due to the riots of communist women…). We had been told that women would not take the trouble to master a difficult policy and that they would never help actively…Whatever your talent – there is a place for you in the Fascist movement!...
>
> *The Blackshirt.* 1 June, 1934 p.4

---

1 Fraddosio M., 1996. The Myth of Mussolini and Fascist Women in the Italian Social Republic (1943-5). *Journal of Contemporary History,* Vol.31, (Jan. 1), p.101

Who's Who of British Women Fascists

Known leading Bristol connected Suffragettes who became prominent members of the British Union of Fascists.

Mary Sophia Allen, (1878-1964). Former Branch Leader of West of England Women's Social and Political Union (WSPU). Commandant of the Women Police Volunteers. Visited Hitler and Franco. Nazi supporter. Speaker and propagandist for BUF. Awarded OBE in 1917.

Mary Richardson, (1882-1961). Friend of Mussolini. WSPU member and arrested in Bristol, July 1914, attempting to present a petition to the King when visiting Bristol. Joined the Labour Party and stood four times as a parliamentary candidate. Joined Mosley's New Party and then his BUF Party. Expelled from the BUF 1935.

Leading Suffragette who became a prominent member of The British Union of Fascists.

Norah Elam (a.k.a. Dacre-Fox), (1878-1961). Imprisoned three times as WSPU member. Independent Parliamentary candidate. Chairman of Chichester Conservatives. Joined BUF in 1934 and stood as parliamentary candidate for Northampton. Popular writer in BUF publications. BUF County Women's Officer for West Sussex. Interned under Defence Regulation 18B. (Hereinafter referred to DR 18B).

Other notable women fascists in South West England.

- Olive Baker from Bath. A school teacher in Germany. Returned to England in 1939. Arrested in 1940 for distributing BU adverts. Cut her wrists while waiting trial and wrote 'Hail Mosley' and 'Heil Hitler' in blood in her cell. Convicted at Bristol Court and given 5 years.
- L. T. Cotton. Member of the BUF in Exeter. Lived in Branscombe. Her name appears on the Home Office Schedule for detention.
- Aileen Diment. Joined the BUF in 1937. Member of the West Dorset Division. She lived in Owermoigne, Dorset as a housewife and distributed BUF literature in the village.[2]
- Lady Laura Kathleen Ismay (nee Clegg). Member of the earlier, British Fascisti Party. Head of the Gloucestershire Women's Unit BF. Wife to General Lord Hastings ("Pug") Ismay (1887-1965). He was Chief of Staff to Winston Churchill's Military Co-ordination Committee (1940-1945), Secretary of State for Commonwealth Relations (1951-1952) and Secretary General of NATO (1952-1954).

2 Boyce L., 2015. *The Bristol Suffragettes Votes of Women Vote Yes!* Silverwood Books.

- Eileen Lyons. Organised a flying club for women members in Gloucestershire and contributed to BUF publications 1936-37.
- I. G. Mereweather. BUF member in 1935. Women's District Officer for Bristol Central.
- Constance E. Mitchell. Women's District Leader for Frome, Bath, Radstock and North Somerset at various times. Interned DR B18.
- D.E. Radford. BUF member in Dorset and lived at 7 High West Street, Dorchester.

Other prominent members of The British Union of Fascists who are mentioned in the text.

- Anne Brock-Griggs. Chief Women's Officer, prominent BUF speaker, served as Women's Propaganda Office. Editor of the Woman's Page in Action. Visited Germany May 1936 for May Day celebrations. June 1936 addressed a meeting of the Women's Institute in Dorset. Prospective BUF Parliamentary candidate for Poplar, East London in 1937. March 1938 spoke at the South Dorset Branch of the National Council of Women at Weymouth. Arrested October 1939 under the Public Order and Defence Reg. 39B, fined £50. Interned with her husband under DR 18B. Died 1960. Author of *Women and Fascism: 10 Important Points* (1936).
- Mrs. H. Carrington-Wood. North West London Organiser for the BUF. Resigned in 1935 over lack of women's representation in the BUF.
- Nellie Driver (1914-1981). Joined BUF with her mother in 1935. By 1936 Women's District Leader of Nelson branch, Lancashire. Frequent speaker for BUF and awarded a bronze medal for her service to the BUF. Mosley thought highly of her and would visit her in the north of England. Detained in October 1940 under DR 18B in Holloway Prison. Transported to Isle of Man detention camp on 16 June 1941. Released in September 1942. Author of *From the Shadows of Exile*, unpublished autobiography and *The Mill*, also autobiographical and unpublished.
- Rotha Beryl Lintorn-Orman (1885-1935). Founded first fascist party in Britain, the British Fascisti Party, May 1923. Frequently in trouble with the law and a very controversial figure. Disliked by Mosley. Died of heavy drinking.
- Lady Ester Makgill. The first leader of the Women's Section. Suspended from BUF in April 1934 due to missing Women's Section funds. July 1937 received six months in prison for fraud using false cheques.

¶ Lady Diana Mosley (nee Mitford) (1910-2003). One of five Mitford sisters, daughters of Lord Redesdale. Met Oswald Mosley in 1932. Visited Hitler with her sister Unity Mitford in 1933. Twice attended the Nuremberg Nazi Parteitag. Attended the Berlin Olympic Games in 1936. Married Oswald Mosley in secret on 6 October 1936 in Berlin at Josef Goebbels' home in Berlin, Hitler being present. 26 July they hosted a party at their London home for Britain's pro-Nazi societies. Arrested 29 June 1940. Detained under DR 18B with Oswald Mosley in Holloway prison until December 1943. Attended the 18B Social Dance held at the Royal Hotel, London in 1945. Published her autobiography *A Life of Contrasts* in 1977. Worked in her later years as a book reviewer for The Evening Standard.

Women Police Volunteers Commandant Mary Sophia Allen standing on the right with her lover Margaret Damer Dawson OBE c.1915.

¶ Lady Katherine Maud 'Ma' Mosley (1874-1948). Sir Oswald's mother. Ran the BUF Women's Branches. Extremely active recruiter for the BUF and very proactive amongst establishment members.

¶ Yolande McShane. Born Liverpool 1916. Joined BUF with her mother in 1935. Women's Branch Leader for Wirral/West Kirby Branch. Then Women's District Inspector of Merseyside. Left BUF in 1937. Joined the Red Cross in 1937 and became a nurse. Worked for the Women's Police Force in Liverpool driving ambulances during WWII. Sent to prison aged 60 in 1976 for bullying her mother in her nursing home (along with nuns), and assisting her mother to commit suicide whilst in nursing home. Author of *Daughter of Evil*. (1980).

¶ Miss I. Sharman-Crawford, BUF member of the Chelsea Branch. Published propaganda articles in *The Blackshirt*.

¶ Gladys Stephenson. Women's Dorset District Leader.

Introduction

Why did fascism appeal to women, and surprisingly also to a small number of former militant suffragettes during the 1920s and 1930s? This is a peculiar conundrum because fascism generally brings forth images of a patriarchal, disciplined, political, macho force, wearing masculine military uniforms and with unquestionable loyalty to the male leader (a cult of the leader).[3] Paradoxically, it is estimated that at one time up to 25% of fascist party members in the 1930s were women. In fact the original fascist party of Britain, the proto British Fascisti party, was founded by a woman, Rotha Lintorn-Orman, on 6th May 1923 and funded by her mother. New Scotland Yard recorded Lintorn-Orman in 1924 as an ex-suffragette.[4] More extraordinary is the fact that many of the foremost admirers and propagandists of the notorious politician and aristocrat Sir Oswald Ernald Mosley (1896-1980) and his British Union of Fascists party were in fact former suffragettes.

This was an era when many political and social organisations were opening up to new ideas, and these places often provided a debating space for new political philosophies. Some women changed their political allegiance from socialism to fascism, while others experimented with new ways of living their lives. These were women who at one time had supported the feminist cause to improve the lives of women so that women could participate in a liberal democratic parliamentary system. A small number of former suffragettes who went on to join the British Union of Fascists in the 1930s had in fact lived in Bristol, or in the surrounding area, and were involved in staging regional meetings, and incidentally, forming a flying club in Gloucestershire to actively promote the British Union of Fascists.

It might be assumed that the suffragettes who joined the British Union of Fascists may have been radicalised through their ill-treatment by the State when imprisoned in Holloway and other regional prisons. During 1912, 240 people were sent to prison for acts against the State while carrying out militant suffragette actions during a campaign of terror instigated by the high command of the Women's Social and Political Union (WSPU) at the height of their campaign for the franchise. Perhaps the women who joined the British Union of Fascists were just astonishingly naïve, genuinely believing a new fascist way of running the country might ultimately achieve better living conditions for ordinary women in British society? Yet, consideration must also be given to

---

3 A cult of the Leader is a cult of personality which arises when an individual (usually male) uses mass media, propaganda or other methods to create an idealised, heroic and sometimes worshipful image.
4 Gottlieb J.V., 2003. *Feminine Fascism: Women in Britain's Fascist Movement.* Tauri. p.316

the fact that some of these women were undoubtedly racist and anti-Semites, though by no means all. Another factor was that these women may have already been committed to ultra-right wing conservatism at heart, naturally progressing to ultra-nationalism and the extreme right following the turmoil of events that overtook Europe in the early twentieth century. This era had seen a bloody and traumatic shift in the stability of the world and ignited a profound sense of nationalism. The outbreak and mayhem of the First World War (WWI), as well as the 1917 Communist Revolution in Russia, galvanised both traditional right and liberal politicians and traumatised aristocratic families to the core, who deeply feared the spread of communism across Europe. Factors such as these may have been why some women were drawn in the first place to the radical arm of the militant wing of the Suffragette movement, the Women's Social and Political Movement (WSPU), led by Emmeline Pankhurst and her daughter Christabel Pankhurst. There were splits over ideology within the WSPU as the movement moved further to the right. Between 1903 and 1906 the WSPU cut off official ties with the Labour Party because Christabel believed that by becoming politically neutral they would attract more middle class women. Christabel argued that the House of Commons would be "more impressed by the demonstrations of the feminine bourgeoisie than of the female proletariat".[5] Emmeline Pankhurst's youngest daughter and ardent activist in the WSPU, Adela Pankhurst Walsh, eventually joined, in 1942, the Australia First Movement, a fascist, pro-Japanese, racist, anti-Semitic movement. She was interned along with her husband as a traitor in 1942 in Australia. In contrast, Sylvia Pankhurst, another daughter of Emmeline, joined the Communist Party in 1920. This clearly demonstrates how in one militant family political leanings had become deeply polarised. Another important clue in analysis is that in 1913 the WSPU appointed the fiercely militant feminist and later fascist, Norah Dacre-Fox (to become known as Norah Elam), as its General Secretary. So, perhaps here lay the roots of the road towards fascism - perhaps these were women who were always fascists at heart and believed that the fight had to be continued outside of the mainstream parties. These are complex issues, but by re-constructing learned academic enquiries, Special Branch records, together with interviews and accounts from the time, it is possible to scrutinise and comprehend the motives of the women and women suffragettes who joined the British Union of Fascists.

5 McNeil S., 2010. *Votes For Ladies. The Suffrage Movement 1867-1918*. Bristol Radical Pamphleteer. Pamphlet #15, 2nd ed.

What is Fascism?

Political theorists have traditionally admitted to having a problem defining fascist ideology, and making it fit into a traditional political ideological framework. This is because the era of twentieth century fascism represented a new ideology that only took on the shape of a serious political party structure during the 1920s.

Fascism is unique as a political movement because it holds attractions to all classes, sexes, ages and political leanings, from ultra-right wing conservatism to extreme left wing ideologies. For example, the Nazi Party under Hitler in Germany, founded in the 1920s and gaining power in 1933, was able to unite competing groups of native German people from all classes and backgrounds. The National Socialists (Nazi Party) did not fit into the usual style of traditional party allegiance at the time, that of membership often being based on class. Nazism appealed to all classes of German citizens, except those on the anti-Nazi ideological left who, as history proved, were to be eradicated in the concentration camps. Hitler described Nazism as being neither of the left or the right but syncretic: politics outside the conventional left-right political spectrum. Fascism and Nazism could be described as a form of extreme authoritarian conservatism that incorporates pseudo-scientific racism. Pseudo-scientific racism typically propagates the idea of a hierarchy of races and thus superior and inferior human sub-species. After World War II the concept of 'race' was comprehensively discredited by empirical research and today the term is not considered to have scientific validity. Lewis, states that 'although fascism is of the centre it is a different animal from Liberalism, which traditionally holds the centre ground. Liberalism respects the democratic process along with the freedom of the individual, known as the doctrine of 'natural rights'. The 'natural rights' must, under a truly liberal-democratic society, be upheld for women as well as for men'.[6]

Fascism on the other hand is strictly authoritarian in character encompassing the notion of the 'organic state' - the individual works for the united progression of the State. Fascism is able to mobilise the population on a revolutionary footing being supremely patriotic, embracing the cult of leader, ultra-romanticised nationalism, imperialist and expansionist by nature, in direct opposition and rejection to both Marxism and free market capitalism, and when necessary, consigning the population to a radical transformation of moral conscience through the vision of a sentimentalised past-nationhood. Fascist doctrine does not believe in the rights of the individual, but rather that

6 Lewis D.S., 1987. *Illusions of Grandeur: Mosley, Fascism and British Society, 1931-1981.* Manchester University Press, p.53

individuals are a collective revolutionary whole working as one for nationalism and to protect the nation from the fears fascism deems from without, such as those who do not follow party doctrine, who are foreigners and those nations beyond empire.

In the twenty-first century we can draw similarities of neo-fascism in organisations such as the so called Islamic State, the Ku Klux Klan in the USA, the Front National in France, and, more recently in the U.K. National Action and the Britain First movement, as well as far eastern dictatorships such as that exists in North Korea. These few examples out of hundreds of far right movements currently established throughout the world are united by the fact they all serve to divide society, race and gender, ultimately to eliminate both men and women who do not choose to follow their creed of intolerant totalitarian ideology.

Former suffragette and British Union of Fascist member, Norah Elam wrote in *Fascist Quarterly*:

> [The] Fascist movement was conducted under strict discipline, and cuts across Party allegiance; its supporters were drawn from every class and Party. Women were to forget self-interest and relinquish petty personal advantages.[7]

During the twentieth century inter-war period, fascist parties were founded in all European countries and in many countries elsewhere in the world, but it was only in Europe, in Italy, and then Germany, that the fascist movement was eventually able to gain power. Mosley aspired to gain political power in Britain after his founding of the British Union of Fascists by attracting young, vigorous men and women from all classes and, obviously, they should be of white, Christian, British heritage, and be willing and able to work on a revolutionary footing, relentlessly for the British Union of Fascists.

A Brief History of the British Union of Fascists

The British Union of Fascists (hereafter to be called the BUF) was founded during the inter-war years in a nation bitterly divided by class conflict and economic turmoil. The Labour Government elected in 1929 had failed the very people it had pledged to help and the National, or coalition, Government of 1931-1940 was seen by radicals of left and right as weak. This was mainly due to the perceived ineptitude of its leaders, faced with the problems of appalling social deprivation, high unemployment, world depression and the ongoing fear

7 Elam N., 1935. 'Fascism, Women and Democracy' *Fascist Quarterly,* Vol.1, p.292

Sir Oswald Ernald Mosley 6th Baronet, former Conservative M.P., a Labour minister and leader of the British Union of Fascists.

of another war in Europe. However, as John Stevens[8] points out it could be said to be to the credit of the National Government that Britain alone of the major European nations preserved a parliamentary democratic system during these years. The big debate about the national government was over appeasement and rearmament: The government can be attacked on the basis that a firmer stand should have been made over Hitler's remilitarisation of the Rhineland in 1936, but can also be defended on the basis that time was needed, that there was a lot of quiet rearmament going on and that the Munich agreement of September 1938 bought Britain a much needed year to prepare for war.

Sir Oswald Mosley dramatically founded the British Union of Fascists in October 1932. Before this Mosley had a brief flirtation with his short lived fascist New Party (NP), (not to be confused with the New Party established in the U.K. in 2003). He founded the right-wing January Club which was a discussion group to attract the establishment to support the BUF. Dorril, states 'MI5 viewed the Club as a powerhouse for the development of Fascist culture'.[9]

8 John Stevens comment to author. August, 2016
9 Dorril S., 2006. *Blackshirt: Sir Oswald Mosley and British Fascism*. Viking

Mosley's NP was launched on 28 February 1931 after Mosley resigned from the Labour Party along with six other Labour MPs. The NP had some respectable supporters including briefly Harold Nicholson (diplomat, writer and later National Labour MP). The NP received £50,000 funding from William Morris the motor manufacturer, later to become Lord Nuffield in 1934, and launched a magazine called *Action*. The NP demonstrated its authoritarian leanings from the beginning, having its own militia called the "Biff Boys" led by the England rugby Captain Peter Howard. After standing candidates in parliamentary elections, none of whom won seats, Mosley toured Europe and this is when he was convinced that fascism was the only way forward for Britain, and indeed Europe. The NP rapidly became more authoritarian and in 1932 Mosley was able to unite various other fascist factions and organisations to merge the NP into his new-found British Union of Fascists. Mosley was to be addressed as 'our Leader'. In 1936 the party name was changed to the British Union as it moved more towards Germany and National Socialism.

Mosley projected himself as a dynamic new force in British politics and by all accounts he was a brilliant and charismatic orator. He was considered a handsome man, a brilliant fencer, for which he won awards. After an education at Winchester College he became an officer cadet at Sandhurst in January 1914. He served in the trenches during the First World War and went on to volunteer for the Royal Flying Corps, flying over enemy lines as an observer in December 1914. He gained his pilot's licence in 1915. Mosley's charm and charisma could well have been an attraction for certain women who may have been drawn towards the BUF. In the autobiographical accounts recorded by Mosley's wife Lady Diana Mosley (nee Mitford), she praises her husband's natural charisma, and she always spoke of him following his death in 1980 with total devotion.[10]

Mosley believed that Britain was heading towards social crisis, believing the government of the day had lost its sense of direction. This belief was supported by prominent capitalists, newspaper owners, high ranking military figurers, former leading WSPU members and sections of the aristocracy, indicating that the party was well funded. On forming the BUF Mosley wrote:

> The Party can be the greatest influence in the modern world for good or evil…the Party must be a Party of men and women dedicated to an idea…its character should be more that of a church than of a political Party.[11]

10 *The Guardian*, 4 March, 1978, p.11
11 *Fascist Quarterly*, 1935

Mosley stated that the BUF was a reactive movement against the 'old gangs' in politics who had let the people down, and the new economics of the fascist corporate state would be the only way forward for a stronger Britain. Corporatism, a means to run the economy and control the population, was at the heart of fascist ideology during the Great Depression advancing into the 1930s. Indeed corporatism was viewed by the BUF as a way to move towards a new politics of the future.

In *Fascist Quarterly* 1935, under the heading 'Fascism and the Old Parties' it was stated:

> The difference between Fascism and [the] socialism of MacDonald or the Conservatism of Eden is a different type of spirit. And this difference of spirit expresses itself in a different type of man – the Blackshirt man. Fascism excludes the possibility of collaboration with any old party because the psychologies of the old parties are irreconcilable with revolutionary Fascism.[12]

Those who supported Mosley came from a wide social/economic spectrum; intellectuals, prominent military officers, ex-service men, farmers, the middle classes, industrial workers, housewives, aristocracy, former suffragettes and newspaper owners, to name a few.[13] They were united in believing that fascism would end international financial ("Jewish") exploitation. The movement, in theory at least, was to be based on a meritocracy for the lower ranks, thereby, uniting the classes and initially, at least, giving equality to women.

In his autobiography Mosley wrote on the emergence of the BUF:

> It is not only necessary to have ideas but also to get them accepted and implemented. I have described the results of this attempt within the old parties, and have reached the point in this story where we went beyond their world and I directly appealed to the mass of the people.[14]

Diana Mosley, his second wife, wrote in her autobiography *A Life of Contrasts*, of the National Government:

> elected at a time of national panic and world-wide slump…a depressing phenomenon…I had the vote but did not use it. Had there been a Lloyd George Liberal in our constituency I should have voted for

12 *Fascist Quarterly*, Vol. 1, July 1935, p.258
13 Edwards R., 2008. *Mosley's Men and Women*. European Social Action. www.oswaldmosley.net
14 Mosley O., 1968. *My Life*. Nelson., p.316

him, but there was not. The over-blown Tory majority and the – as it seemed to young people then – absurd figure of Ramsay MacDonald pretending to lead it as prime minister [was] a despairingly inadequate combination…Radical reform was imperative.[15]

Diana Mosley's comment on the views of the younger generation are very relevant as the fascist movement was seen by Oswald Mosley as a new beginning for Britain – a new way to govern – led by a fascist male demigod - who was to lead from the top down. Also, she believed in the proposed autocratic and political corruptible system of corporations that could be manipulated by Mosley to secure domination over the population. In her autobiography, Diana Mosley sheds next to no light on her involvement in the party apparatus. The book, while revealing the extent of her undoubted admiration of Adolf Hitler, includes accounts of her numerous visits to Germany and Italy with her sister Unity Mitford, but is sparse over her personal involvement in the development of the BUF. Most disappointingly, other than recollections of a few fascist social engagements, there is no mention of the involvement of the other women members in the party - many of whom were her personal friends. The reasons for these omissions were to protect her friends and to brush over the totalitarian nature of her husband's leadership and her involvement in the BUF.

During a speech made in Bath to announce that a BUF branch was to be formed in the city, it was reported in the *Bath Weekly Chronicle and Herald* (Oct 14, 1933), that Mr Cuming, chief propaganda officer of the BUF, made clear that "Fascism in Britain aims to establish the Corporate State, a political economic unit in which class warfare, strikes, lock-outs, etc., are abolished; we believe in an Empire of economic union." This was an unambiguous message to the political left directed at the Trades Unions and other workers' organisations that the BUF would find another way to manage the State and its creed would not tolerate socialism.

Meanwhile during the following year, in Bristol, the BUF branch was busy planning to entertain German and Italian fascists at its headquarters located on Park Street. The *Western Daily and Bristol Mirror* reported on the 25th May, 1934 in dramatic fashion, 'Nazis and Italian Fascists Visit to Blackshirts in Bristol Last Night'. They reported that fifty German Nazis and Italian fascists paid a surprise visit to the Bristol local branch of the BUF on Park Street after arriving by boat at Avonmouth and were entertained to supper. There were cheers for Hitler, Mosley and Mussolini before they left.[16]

15 Mosley D., 1977. *A Life of Contrasts*. Hamish Hamilton. p.94
16 The author believes that the BUF Headquarters in Bristol was at the Hamilton Rooms on Park Street ironically the same street that had once been the home of the WSPU Headquarters.

BUF Women's Section meeting, perhaps at London Headquarters (Mary Richardson stands at the back).

The British Union of Fascists: Ideology and Women

Mosley's vision of a fascist Britain included women and he desperately wanted to recruit women activists into the party's new regional branches. In order to attract women, announcements began to appear in the official party newspaper, *The Blackshirt*, calling for regional meetings solely for the attention of women. A 'women only' meeting was advertised to be held in the Gloucestershire area in June, 1934:

> The Blackshirt speaker will be a woman, and the meeting will be stewarded entirely by women members.[17]

Owing to increasing membership in Plymouth, fascists opened a Plymouth section headquarters on the city's Millbay Road as early as 1933 in the former Empire Services Club. The building was converted to house a canteen and a gymnasium 'with capable instructors present that would be available for the

17 *The Blackshirt.* 29 June, 1934

training and recreation of members.' More alarming the BUF stated that the building would also house a room [for] courts of enquiry, courts-martial and proceedings of a disciplinary nature! A women's section was also organised in Plymouth as female members already existed in other towns nearby according to press reports of the time.[18]

Furthermore, the fascist press often contained articles supporting the women's cause for greater rights in society. One such article written in 1934 by a Miss I. Sharman-Crawford, BUF member of the Chelsea Branch, that appeared in *The Blackshirt*, goes to great lengths to link the fascist movement with the continuation of the suffragette fight using bold statements such as: 'Fascism takes up the work for those first pioneers for women's rights, and carries it to its logical and final achievement'.[19] Ironically the party professed to stand for equal opportunities across the sex divide in order to attract women, which is directly in conflict with the very nature of fascist doctrine, being dominated by a patriarchal leadership that saw women as child bearers and homemakers. When pressed on this contradiction the party's propagandists would argue that the British Anglo-Saxon fascist way was culturally distinct from Italian fascism or National Socialism in Germany because Britain was not overly influenced by Catholicism. Policy links and deals were made between Mussolini and the Catholic Church in Italy, notably education policy and banning contraception. The Roman Catholic Church had far less influence on Nazism in Germany.

On its foundation the BUF did support the right of all women to work outside the home. But increasingly the BUF emphasised that women were victims of a mainly Jewish capitalist elite who exploited women through a sweated labour market because they worked for less pay than men. Disregarding the racism element of BUF propaganda, it could not be disputed at the time that many women were (and still are in many cases), exploited as cheap labour within female employment opportunities. The over-riding theme in *The Blackshirt* articles was to consistently lead the reader to the 'truth' of fascist philosophy i.e. the 'natural' place for a woman is to be married, with children and with an honourable man supporting the family. The role of the woman as housewife was to be elevated to an honorary position through membership of Mosley's vision of a 'Corporation for Married Women', the 23rd Corporation, (later to be known as the Domestic Corporation). Alexander Raven Thompson (c.1934), writing in his pamphlet, *The Corporate State* made the argument that the failure in democracy to end economic turmoil, causing great suffering, should be replaced by a form of government based not on geographical regions

18 *The Western Morning News and Daily Gazette*. 16 Sept. 1933
19 Berry P. & Bishops A. (eds), 1985 *Testament of a Generation: The Journalism of Vera Brittain and Winifred Holtby*. London. pp.84-86

but by occupational groups. These groups, or corporations, would bring together workers, employers and consumers. The housewife and women in general would get representation in the corporation relevant to her. For example, the Farming/ Agricultural Corporation is an example of where womankind would be represented being the purchaser of the family food. Durham, rightly concludes that the BUF was somewhat unpredictable on women's issues. He states that 'Contrary to conventional wisdom, the BUF, rather than denouncing feminism, claimed to be compatible with it.' And, 'Enthusiastic woman propagandists, some with a feminist background were eager to persuade women of the virtues of its position.'[20]

The origins of fascist corporatism are generally associated with Benito Mussolini. The government, or privately in some cases, would manage all sectors of the economy through controlled organisation. The corporations might be called trade unions or employer corporations to give them an air of neutrality from the state and should in theory lead to an idealised harmony amongst all social classes. But, as this system was to be introduced by a totalitarian state, non-elected state officials would manage the corporations. In reality the corporations would become corrupt because the system was used to reduce opposition to party policy and to ultimately reward political loyalty. Mosley believed that through a system of corporatism he had found a radical solution to Britain's economic problems. Writing in his book *The Greater Britain* in 1932, Mosley declared that 'original corporate thinking belongs to Mussolini'. Mosley further expands:

> It is this machinery of central direction which the Corporate State is designed to supply...It envisages, as its name implies, a nation organized as a human body. Every part fulfils its function as a member...The whole body is generally directed by the central driving brain of government.[21]

Generally, governments of the time encouraged married women to stay at home in order to create employment for men. But, the difference with fascist rhetoric is that women were given a pious status in the fascist press, thereby endorsing and exposing the BUF's true, hidden policy on women's rights and freedoms. Furthermore, it was presumed by the fascist press that women who had to work suffered a 'stigma' from this form of exploitation (having to work outside the home), and would therefore prefer to stay at home. To stay at home was interpreted as:

20 Durham M., 1998. *Women and Fascism.* Routledge, p.48
21 Mosley O., 2012. *The Greater Britain.* Black House Publishing Ltd. p.26

the freedom to follow the dictates of their own hearts in choosing whether they will work on an equal base with men, or stay in their homes and live the lives that their womanhood would have them lead.[22]

Female employment in 1920s and 1930s Britain was also intrinsically bound up with the issue of male pride. The status of the working wife in the 1930s had stigma attached to it, inferring that a man was not able to provide adequately for his family. Fascist doctrine of encouraging (later to become forced under Italian fascism and German Nazism), women back into the home would have completely halted the evolution of female emancipation in Britain. The economic crisis of 1929 had enormous consequences for women workers in Nazi Germany; women paid for the economic crash by being dismissed from work in professions such as medicine, science and teaching employed many women in Germany at this time. Both fascist Italy and Nazi Germany decreed that in any organisation, whether state or private, the proportion of women employed must not exceed ten percent. What is more, in Germany, women were also restricted from attending higher education, with their fees being doubled.[23]

After founding the BUF it was anticipated by Mosley that the significance of recruiting women into the party was that women were vocal and capable of influencing the masses. Mosley had witnessed the capabilities of militant women campaigning with immense passion to fight for their recognised place in society through enfranchisement. The Women's Social Political Union (WSPU) was ultimately successful - although it took the tragedy of the First World War (WWI) for women to eventually gain the vote in Britain.

Some historians have argued that the WSPU showed all the elements of a para-military force. The WSPU was led from the top down through a strict female hierarchy, employing highly trained self-defence tactics by means of ju-jitsu. Women members were trained in self-defence to make them feel confident; to fight off violent attacks from the police as occurred on Black Friday,[24] as well as to raise their self-esteem and physical stamina. The suffragettes also had to endure torture while in prison, through forced feeding, the effects from which some never fully recovered their health. The WSPU's newspaper was sold on street corners – the women sometimes under attack and being spat at - wearing

22 *The Blackshirt*, 1936
23 Macciocchi M. A., 1979. Female Sexuality in Fascist Ideology. *Feminist Review.* No.1, p.72
24 Black Friday occurred on the 18th November, 1910. Three hundred unarmed women marched on parliament demanding the vote. Two hundred of these women were man handled and assaulted by plain clothes policemen. This was a public relations disaster for the government. A few days later, on being released from prison, Mary Clarke, Emmeline Pankhurst's sister died.

the colours (a uniform of sorts) of the Suffragette movement. Training classes were also regularly run by the WSPU to teach members how to run meetings and speak effectively in public. Critically, Mosley required the character of the militant female spirit to boost his small party at local elections – women who would use their vote to give the party the power they craved – women who knew how to speak in public, and, most importantly, women trained to confront often violent opposition to the BUF. Comparisons have been made with the actions of Irish Nationalists at the time where women were seen as more effective in being able to deescalate violence from opponents.

Six months after the formation of the BUF, the Women's Section was created in March 1933. There is little written material regarding the early days of the organisation of the Women's Section. However, the first leader of the Women's Section was Lady Makgill, who was later dismissed for stealing party funds. The second leader of the Women's Section was Mosley's mother, Lady Katherine Maud 'Ma' Mosley who by all accounts had a firm hold over her son's private life and his political career.

Mosley's creed of Fascism was loosely based on Mussolini's Italian fascist party – The Partito Nazionale Fascista. Fascist policy of the Italian Corporate State was at the centre of Mosley's commitment to re-organise economic and government control of the State. Essentially the Women's Corporation was to offer women equality in the work place and, strangely, in the home through a Domestic Corporation, via strictly stratified committees working under a non-democratic parliament. But what did the Italian fascist state and Germany's Nazi political system have in store for women under this system? This is of particular relevance when considering why the BUF appealed to some women and not to others, women who had been suffragettes, who were tortured by force feeding whilst in prison, who had stood alongside liberal minded women so that all women from any race, creed or class could participate in their democratic right to vote.

Conventional fascist doctrine dictates that women are to occupy the private sphere (the home) to produce and care for the needs of the children and men for the common good of the Nation. This doctrine also had the desired effect of excluding women from employment in order to create full employment for men, particularly following the WWI. Fascism is inherently masculine by nature, run according to a strict code of patriarchal hierarchy; a society where the men traditionally go out to work and perform for the good of the nation by participating in the public sphere. Mussolini prescribed that women could work, but only within positions that traditionally would not be a threat to male employment such as in the role of spinster school teacher, interior decorator, florist, landscape gardener, or perhaps as a dance instructor.

Hitler also made it apparent that women were to play no active role in public life under Nazism. Women in Nazi Germany were removed from the electoral list and were excluded from positions of responsibility within the party and state – measures which were to have a drastic effect on their lives. However, after 1936, women in Nazi Germany were allowed once again to take up employment in the armament factories due to the fact that male unemployment had come down to an acceptable level and women were needed to work in these factories. This, though, was not the long-term ideological goal of the Nazis, but rather that it was simply that women were required temporarily in the work place to bolster the war effort. During a speech that Hitler made on 8th September 1934, he stated that 'National Socialists have for years guarded against the intrusion of women into political life and we do not consider it right that a woman should intrude into the world of man'.[25]

Goebbels, Hitler's Minister of Propaganda from 1933 to 1945, once said "While man masters life, woman masters the pots and pans".[26] As the bearers of children, German women received praise from the Nazi propaganda machine for their role in producing the future 'warriors' of the Fatherland. This was in keeping with traditional fascist ideology of an Expansionist Empire or territorial expansionism mirrored by Mosley's dogma of the further expansion of the British Empire to further advance growth for the British economy. In Germany repression of women also took place in education, with the emphasis on training girls for motherhood, domestic science and biology (to train as nurses), at the cost of their academic ability. Also, interestingly, slimming was discouraged under Nazism as it was considered not only vain, but had the added danger of possibly lowering the birth rate. Mosley supported this opinion. Fascist policy of social reconstruction of gender was contained within the philosophy of the BUF, but was played down in order to attract women members who were seen as being very valuable to the movement since gaining the right to vote.

Mosley's writings appear to indicate that he sought to promote the interests of women by allowing them to have active engagement at grass-roots level, but importantly, a restricted role within the upper hierarchy of the movement. However, this is an ambiguous picture. Mosley wrote in *Fascist Week*, January 1934, that it was a falsehood that women were repressed in Italy and Germany, and in any event British fascism would pursue its own path. It [the BUF] did not regard 'women purely as mothers of the race'.[27] An article in *The Blackshirt*, that appeared just five months later, entitled 'Women and the Corporate State', argued that the professions which Mussolini prescribes being appropriate

25 Guirdham A., *Against Pity*. Anglia Ruskin University Articles Collection p.7
26 *Ibid.*
27 *Fascist Week,* 12-18 January, 1934

for women to engage in i.e. teaching, floristry etc. are to be encouraged for 'educated' women in Britain so that they are not in competition with men. What Mosley fails to acknowledge is that these were middle-class occupations, ignoring the plight of most working class women who were often working in poor conditions on low wages. Was Mosley proposing here that only middle class women were to be able to engage in work so that he did not alienate former suffragettes and with them the middle class vote?

Early on in the movement's right-wing progress, Mosley established the role of women in Britain in the event of the BUF gaining power - that being the honour of bearing children for both men and the Fascist State. The fascist movement was seen by Mosley as a new beginning for Britain – a new way to lead – with himself as a fascist male demigod who led from the top down – the fascist way. As can be noted in 1934, when Mosley wrote:

> 'Motherhood and the joy of carrying on the race', this was to be acknowledged within the Corporate State as 'one of the greatest of human and racial functions, to be honoured and encouraged.

To support BUF policy the party published in 1937, seven propositions to women:
1. Education for women to seek advice before the birth of their children.
2. More clinics, of a more efficient and attractive design.
3. More women doctors, who may be preferred by patients.
4. Better training, pay and hours for midwives.
5. More specialised training in obstetric work for doctors.
6. Improvement and extension of local hospitals to provide more maternity beds, and also facilities for training doctors and midwives.
7. Convalescent homes and an extended home help service enabling mothers to recuperate fully after the birth of their babies.[28]

Although commendable health provisions for women of child bearing age these aspirations were about establishing an anti-feminist creed for women by driving them back into the home; making procreation more attractive and less dangerous; and rewarding women who followed the party line. The party was clearly shifting further to the right, towards National Socialism and this would mean that women were to be inevitably pushed out of the higher ranks of the BUF.

28 The Problem of the Woman Worker: National Socialism Will Solve It. *The Blackshirt*, No. 146, 23 Jan. 1937, cited in Gottlieb J.V. op. cit.

The Attraction of the British Union of Fascists to Women

The first woman speaker at a fascist rally in Bristol was Mrs Anne Brock-Griggs, propaganda officer for the BUF. She addressed a meeting on Tuesday 18th February, 1936 at the Hamilton Rooms, Park Street, Bristol, where the author believes the Bristol BUF Headquarters were located. She spoke about the role of women in the BUF declaring that women would have a more:

> favourable [role] than under the democratic system. Women would have absolute equality of representation, a true voice in the government of the country, particularly in regard to social reforms which were so essential, allowed to occupy any position in the State, any career would be open to them, but on equal terms with men - that was equal pay for equal work…those principles would do away with cheap woman labour in industry and men would replace them, but a woman would hold a position if worthy of it…they would not allow sweated labour in England. (*Western Daily Press and Bristol Mirror*, Feb. 19, 1936)

These were the words of a true fascist feminist, but how does this statement stand up when examining the BUF's social policy envisioned for women and the long term aims of the BUF? Women were to find themselves increasingly marginalised as the decade moved forward with the BUF aligning itself more and more with Hitler's Nazi and anti-feminist policies directed from Berlin.

From the early formation of the BUF, propaganda was directed at women though the BUF's weekly publications that were sold to the public on the streets by women members. A directive from the BUF headquarters reads:-

> It cannot be too strongly urged that women Fascists should take every opportunity offered both at Headquarters and at the local centres, to train as speakers...canvassers...[Women] who spread Fascism privately among friends and acquaintances.

This was a call for women of all classes and backgrounds to join and work publicly to bring about a fascist government. But surely this call for action is rather bewildering? Conventional fascist ideology expressly epitomises a movement that is undoubtedly patriarchal, misogynistic and to bring about an autocratic system of government controlled by men. Fascism is by nature infinitely authoritarian and always encompasses a strict division of gender roles both within society and party, a sex-segregation – the private and the public spheres both proclaim how women and men are to live out their lives. However, Mosley understood the need to have women among his ranks.

Feminists moved away from women's groups after the franchise was gained for women aged twenty-one and over in 1928. Some women were naturally drawn into different political parties, welcomed by leaders who by now had recognised that women had their uses within the party machine - and the BUF was no exception. The ever astute Mosley realised that the BUF needed women to politicise the home – the internal weapon that could convert both man and child. He needed women who were trained, found an attraction in wearing a uniform, and were already radicalised to take on conventional politics. Such women would make ideal militant activists for the BUF, and Mosley in recognition planned a 'monster' women's peace campaign. On February 28th, 1934, at Holborn, London, Chief Women's Officer, Anne Brock-Griggs, along with Commandant Mary Allen, former suffragette connected with Bristol and Olive Hawks, addressed the first ever significant BUF indoor meeting which was organised entirely for women. Women were now seemingly at the heart of the organisation.

The process of political socialisation is complex for both genders and is influenced by factors such as: class; parental political influence, education, and life experiences. These influences are registered consciously and unconsciously by individuals and might incorporate feelings of insecurity for self and nation especially during times of political uncertainty and upheaval. Societal perception of change in the political power of women would have been a strong influence during the 1930s. In recognition of women over 21 years of age having been given the vote in 1928, women members of the BUF were granted, initially, an active role in the development strategy of the party. For example, women were allowed to make speeches at rallies and to work as stewards at meetings for which they received 'special training'. Women were seen very much in the public sphere, acting tough, holding their own, wearing para-military uniforms, and often on the front line when faced with staunch, and sometimes violent, opposition from communist opponents and others.

Fear of a second war in Europe constituted another of the movement's attractions for women, particularly in the late 1930s. A large proportion of male membership was made up of war veterans who naturally felt revulsion for the concept of war. The same can be said of the female membership and ex-suffragettes who had also played their role in the First World War as ambulance drivers, nurses and workers in armament factories. Three former women BUF members interviewed by Stephen Cullen in the 1980s gave the same reasons as the men for their motives for joining the BUF, that of a sense of patriotism and betrayal of the people who suffered so much during WWI. The BUF was against a new war with Germany and offered a 'dynamic new force' to oppose another war in Europe. Women members, including former suffragette Mary Allen, went to Germany on a peace mission paid for by the BUF.

One woman interviewed by Cullen stated that she 'admired Unity Mitford for her courage'. (Unity Mitford was the sister of Lady Diana Mosley). These women saw the BUF as the only party which was dedicated to avoiding another European war. In the period 1938 to 1940, issues of *The Blackshirt,* apart from the virulent anti-Semitic articles that appeared, contained dedicated articles promoting an intellectual argument against war with Germany. The articles attempted to convince its readership that the German people had 'never had it so good' as they had now under Hitler. Idealised pictures appeared of sun-tanned, well fed German children collecting flowers in the fields in order to depict a nation at peace with itself. The pictures appeared next to those of British slums portraying a dislocated Britain with weak leadership, at the mercy of "Jewish finance".

The BUF's pacifist element in its ideology was based on a patriotic theme, but also played on an anti-war feeling of unease within the general population. Mosley consistently argued that Britain should only be concerned with empire and should only go to war if the empire itself was under attack from a foreign force. This opinion was by no means confined to fascists but was widely held in government circles prior to the outbreak of war.

Meanwhile in Bristol on the night of 10th March, 1936 the *Western Daily Press and Bristol Mirror* (11 March, 1936) reported on the front page

'Wild Scenes at Bristol Fascist Meeting – Interrupters Ejected by Black-Shirted Stewards'. A large crowd had gathered outside Colston Hall, Bristol, to demonstrate against the BUF rally that evening, attended by over 1,500 people. Mosley himself was to have spoken but at the last minute, fearing a riot, his deputy officer, Mr William Joyce,[29] BUF director of propaganda, addressed the meeting instead. The meeting did not go well; Joyce was constantly interrupted from the gallery. Joyce responded with "we will teach interrupters such a lesson that they will never come back to repeat their bad-mannered practices in one of our halls. If you want to know why we use violence we should never be able to pay out [such] cause before the people unless we were granted freedom of speech." "Rubbish", said a woman in the gallery and 'her remark was received with loud applause'. Joyce responded "Nothing would be more degrading than it should be necessary for me to enter into controversy with a lady, evidently determined to make a nuisance of herself." According to the newspaper report:

> A woman's voice interrupted again, and the women stewards were told to remove her. A struggle then ensued between the woman and women stewards. Eventually they released her grip on the rails in front of her and removed her, a gangway being forced through the crowd by the police.

Women were certainly active in opposing the BUF in Bristol. 'An ugly situation' was reported on the front page of the *Western Daily Press and Bristol Mirror* (2 June, 1934) after the police called for the Fascists to end a street corner meeting in Bedminster. A clash occurred at the corner of Guinea Street, Bedminster on the 1st June, 1934 when members of the BUF were heckled by members of the Bristol Unemployed Movement.[30] Men and women were reported heckling BUF speakers on the street corner. When the Fascists marched back to their headquarters on Park Street they were followed by a large crowd and a fight broke out on the street outside St Mary Redcliffe Church. Several men were injured and the police stepped in to protect the Fascists. Again the crowd was separated by the police at Bristol Bridge and the Fascists were given protection by the police so they could continue to their headquarters.

29 William Joyce and his wife Margaret fled to Berlin in 1939. Worked for Nazis as chief English language radio commentator, broadcasting Nazi propaganda under the name Lord Haw-Haw. He was hanged at Wandsworth Prison, London in 1946 on three counts of High Treason.
30 Believed to be referring to the National Unemployed Workers' Movement (NUWM), the main organisation opposing unemployment and the 'cuts'. Source: Backwell D. & Ball R., *Bread or Batons? Unemployed Workers Struggles in 1930s Bristol.* Bristol Radical Pamphleteer. Pamphlet #10. 2012

The Battle of the Shirts: Fashion for Fascism

Fashion, a common theme for the press and a feminist issue, was a key element in attracting certain men and women members into the BUF. Even today female politicians still attract interest over what they are wearing, and how their choice of dress may project a certain image. Following the creation of the women's sections, the party decided that women members needed a militaristic style of uniform. This in part was to construct the fascist ideal of womanhood and at the same time to attract new male recruits. This era of the BUF is known as 'the battle of the shirts' because the uniform was a huge attraction to many women members. In 1933 *The Fascist Week* ran a propaganda piece to thank those women who had attracted men to join the movement: 'Fascism in Britain knows that it is a woman's influence that has converted so many of its male members'.[31] Mosley followed, once again, the visions of Mussolini and his ideal military style uniform for the fascist woman; to be cut as a military uniform, to unite and appeal to women members, later to be called 'black blouses'. The Italian code of dress for women consisted of a dark grey suit, with short breeches, stockings, black boots, a grey Alpine hat and the inevitable black shirt. Mussolini had become a dictator of fashion and Mosley was soon to follow his lead. The British fascist female uniform was a grey skirt, black shirt/blouse, a black beret with short close-cropped hair and wearing the party badge. It was against regulations for women to be dressed in trousers or wear lipstick while on duty. When women were acting as stewards at meetings they wore slightly different black shirts with collars like Mosley's - a fencing style shirt. It was also advised for women to wear black underwear to save embarrassment if clothing was torn during fights! However, as recalled, in the oral account of Ray Webber, that at the women only Blackshirt meeting he attended, the women were in fact wearing brown skirts.

While the ideal male fascist was to have firm chiselled lines, to have vast courage and strength, along with loyalty to leader, women were also to display these attributes equally described as being healthy, charming, attractive, intelligent and sober. But most importantly – they should pay attention to their motherliness:

> Nothing silly about these women. They are nothing if not practical…
> as the happy carefree way in which they made themselves at home,
> was so refreshing after one has had their fill of the simpering little
> brats that democracy and Jewish films have produced.[32]

31 *The Fascist Week,* No.2. 17 Nov. 1933
32 *The Blackshirt,* Women Enjoy the Camp. No. 227, 4 Sept. 1937

Feminist Irene Clephane on discussing the progression of women's freedom in the early 1930s noted:

> Amongst the oddest spectacles of the day is that of young women dressed in black shirts, standing on the pavement edges offering for sale the literature of the Fascists, one of whose aims is to deprive women of the very freedom which makes it possible to stand unmolested as they do.[33]

Later in his life Mosley believed that the BUF para-military uniform was a propaganda disaster. Due to constant pitched battles between pro and anti-fascist groups in the East End of London it was decided by the government to ban the wearing of military-style uniforms. The general consensus in the press was that the Blackshirts were in fact a private army which was causing provocation. The government rushed through the Public Order Act of 1936 to control extremist political movements, and in the case of the BUF to take away their identity. Mosley's reaction was to declare that the BUF was being discriminated against with Mosley himself continuing to wear his uniform at public meetings, defying the government, and challenging them to declare what a 'uniform' consisted of. Members did continue to wear their uniforms at private meetings and wore armlets in public which displayed the party symbol. Several members were prosecuted for wearing para-military uniform in public, but the government chose to ignore Mosley's personal protest in order to deny him further publicity.

British Union of Fascists: Women and anti-Semitism

A fascinating recording of David Frost interviewing Oswald Mosley exists on *YouTube* (15 Nov 1967). Frost asked Mosley if he was anti-Semitic, quoting from many of Mosley's Jew baiting 1930s speeches. Mosley answered "we were in a fight with the Jews or many Jews I won't say all Jews, a tremendous fight! And I hit them as they were hitting me! With everything I got….I had to organise the Blackshirt movement to keep order….they came out to provoke a world war!… Our meetings were attacked…" He denied ever being an anti-Semite and blamed the Jews for attacking his meetings in the East End of London – the Jewish Quarter where the Blackshirts marched and organised meetings.

BUF official racial policy stated that minorities were to be excluded from public life in order to unite the nation through the doctrine of racial purity.

33 Durham M., 1992. Gender and the British Union of Fascists. *Journal of Contemporary History*. Sage Publications Ltd. Vol.27, No.3 (Jul). p.515

White, British women, being the bearers of children, were to play a vital role if such a doctrine was to be successful. Many of the BUF's women members were openly anti-Semitic. One woman member stated '[I] hated them [Jews] with every breath in my body'. It was reported in the *Jewish Chronicle* that [BUF] women 'adopted a more hysterical anti-Jewish attitude than did their men-folk'.

The Western Daily Press and Bristol Mirror reported on the front page, in 1934, questions posed to Mosley during a BUF rally at the Albert Hall, London:

> Sir Oswald Mosley replied to the Jewish question: "that under fascism Jews would have to put the interests of Britain, and not of Jewry, first. Jews were not admitted to the organisation because they had declared themselves hostile to it, and it would be folly to take in such people".

It was also reported that as the meeting ended 'a young Scotsman in the gallery came to blows with a Fascist. The Blackshirt fell down some stairs and received slight injuries'. As this report noted it is not just members of the Jewish community who opposed the BUF and its racist policies but a broad cross-section of the British public.

Two years later *The Western Daily Press and Bristol Mirror* reported on 11 March, 1936:

> Whilst addressing a large meeting in Bristol, Mr W. Joyce, Propaganda Officer for the BUF, stated that [under] "fascism the Jew would be treated as a foreigner with the privileges of every other well-behaved foreigner. Those who proved to be undesirable would be transported to Palestine".

This statement supposes that British subjects with Jewish ancestry were to be denied their legal rights as British citizens, just as they were being denounced in Nazi Germany at the time.

The questions at this point include the following: were some former suffragettes anti-Semitic? Did they join the BUF to fight the mythical Jewish plot against Britain? And, what part did fascist women play in condoning Mosley's anti-Semitic dogma? Undoubtedly some former suffragettes were anti-Semitic, why else would they have aligned themselves to the BUF? It is clear that racism is never just a minority male attribute because women are just as likely to be racist. As Gottlieb so eloquently wrote:

motherly love was turned into motherly hate. Victims, and their Jew-baiting activities, their appeals to motherly protectiveness and their fear-mongering drove the anti-Semitic campaign at every turn. In its reaction to [socialist feminism] feminine fascism transformed motherly love into motherly hate.[34]

Several of the leading former suffragettes made public speeches denouncing the perceived over-influence of European Jewry and by implication the banking sector. Anna Brock Griggs spoke of and blamed the "corrupt Jewish landlords and Jewish government ministers" as to why East End London slum clearances had not proceeded. In 1936 she wrote in *Action* and *Fascist Quarterly* 'Fascism does not need the poisoned blood money of aliens [Jews] to rehouse British people', and warned of the 'evil force of finance, which flourishes as weeds do in the gardens they destroy'.

In *Rules of the Game; Beyond the Pale*[35], Mosley's son Nicholas Mosley, describes how his father's fascist speeches were to result in racial attacks on East End Jewish residents:

The next Sunday in the East End there was a 'victory' parade by anti-Fascists; the police now had to make baton-charges to make a way for them…A gang of about 200 pro-Fascist and mostly teenage youths ran down Mile End Road smashing Jewish shop windows and attacking anyone who might be thought to look Jewish: a hairdresser and a four-year-old girl were reportedly thrown through a plate-glass window. British Union officials denied responsibility for this; they said as usual that such behaviour was strictly against orders.

The evidence suggests that former suffragettes who joined the BUF were predominantly racists and anti-Semites. They made speeches, and wrote articles in the Fascist press denouncing Jews for paying low wages and low sexual morals. These were intelligent, educated women who fully understood the racism of fascist ideology.

Yolande McShane, a woman Blackshirt, was eventually to turn hostile towards the BUF as is shown in the extract below, written later in her life, where she describes her growing unease and concern about Hitler and fascism:

34 Gottlieb J.V. op. cit
35 Mosley Nicholas, 1991. *Rules of the Game; Beyond the Pale: Memoirs of Sir Oswald Mosley and Family*. Dalkey Archive Press

His atrocities against the countries he occupied and against the Jews had sickened me…I realised too that in joining the Blackshirts I had been totally misled, they were after all linked with Hitler's politics.[36]

Racism is at the heart of fascist ideology. By incorporating a strict code of racial hierarchy, a fundamental element as to how Fascists establish a fascist state, racism is rationalised through the mythical evils of the *folk-devil* - which keeps the State and population on a revolutionary footing.

In their words: Women who joined the British Union of Fascists

Accounts of why women joined the movement and their expectations for a fascist government regularly appeared in the Fascist press. These newspapers included *Action, The Blackshirt,* and *Fascist Weekly*, and in the early days *Woman Fascist*, a publication solely aimed at women members as a propaganda tool to recruit new women members. Many of the articles written in these publications were supposedly written by women and had titles such as 'Why Fascism Appeals to Me', signed by 'An Ordinary Woman'. It is probable that these articles were produced from the party's active propaganda machinery to encourage women to join. The articles illustrate a clear program of indoctrination and training for women recruits such as accounts of training weekends, a martial arts training, a study school, and photographs of women enjoying BUF summer camps. The articles were also written with the aim of enhancing the movement's respectability to encourage the middle classes to join. Commentaries that appeared in *The Blackshirt* always followed an ideological pathway for the expected role for women members. In September 1934 the 'Women's Section' of the party was for the first time given extra editorial space in *The Blackshirt*.

The small amount of research undertaken by academics suggests that women from all classes of society joined the BUF, which is a common characteristic of fascism and the concept of the fascist organic state. Lady Mosley, during an interview with *The Guardian* newspaper in 1989, stated that:

[there were] a bevy of high-society hostesses who ran pro-Nazi salons. They included: Lady Cunard who was a close friend of Wallis Simpson, wife of the abdicated former King Edward VIII, and who had access through her to the Prince of Wales; Dame Maggie Greville DBE, who had the ear of Sir John Simon, the Foreign Secretary, Lady Astor, and

36 *The Star* newspaper, McShane Yolanda. *Daughter of Evil.* 1980 pp.30-33

Lady Londonderry DBE, whose friend, Ribbentrop, was known in those circles as the Londonderry Herr.[37]

(Lady Londonderry's husband, Lord Londonderry was also a Nazi sympathiser, at least before the outbreak of war and possibly afterwards; his story is told in Ian Kershaw, *Making Friends with Hitler*, London 2004).

Four Women for Mosley by Cullen,[38] is a comprehensive survey focusing solely on female membership. The study was compiled in the mid-1980s and focused on ideology, membership and the meetings that the women attended. Cullen states that his main contacts were former women BUF members who had maintained an informal friendship following Second World War (WWII) after having made initial friendships whilst in prison and WWII internment camps. They were part of an old Mosleyite members' association – Friends of Oswald Mosley. The four women that Cullen interviewed, although representing only a tiny fraction of the total female membership of the BUF, nevertheless shed a valuable insight into their experiences of the movement, as well as their motivations for joining the Party. The women claimed that they joined the BUF for reasons of patriotism, social concerns and fear of another world war. Here are extracts of their testimonies:

Jane: [I was] deeply patriotic, though not extrovert flag waving type, and much that was happening in [the] early 1930s appeared to reject this deep feeling of the majority as somehow out of date. I believed also the state of deprivation in large sections of our society both locally and nationally was an insult to human dignity, and a betrayal of my parents' generation who had suffered so much in the First War to 'make a land fit for heroes to live in'. The BUF was the only movement which appeared to have the will and honesty to face all the problems and made attempt to change them while keeping all that was best of our traditions.

Lorna: I felt it [the general situation] wanted something new and dynamic, not just the old part of politics. I suppose I was a bit of a socialist, because obviously you want better conditions when I saw these back-to-back houses. I got a job in a special school, for defective children….and I used to go in the bus sometimes collecting the children, and some of the conditions they came from, you know,

---

37 Mikardo I., 1989. *The Guardian Supplement.* 11 Feb., pp.6-7
38 Cullen S., 1996. Four Women for Mosley: Women in the British Union of Fascists, 1932-1940. *Oral History.* Vol.24 No.1. *Political Lives* (Spring) pp.49-59

Women fascists saluting Oswald Mosley.

it was quite an eye-opener for me. And then I found out where the bookshop and the headquarters of the British Union was, as I said, I felt that I wanted to do something *quickly*.[39]

Cullen's research glimpses a rare insight into why these two women, from different political backgrounds, but both being deeply patriotic, joined the BUF. They clearly wanted improvements in society and felt genuinely let down by inter-war governments who failed to enhance living conditions. The women were interested in the political landscape of the day and clearly felt a collective sense of social and political betrayal. The women were also fervent nationalists just as some of the former suffragettes caused the militant arm of the WSPU to split into right wing pro-war and left wing anti-war factions, over the threat of imperialist Germany in 1913.

Conversely, another woman who Cullen interviewed had an entirely different motive for joining the BUF. Pauline was eighteen years of age when she joined the BUF in 1932 and confessed to having 'no political bent at all'

39 *Ibid*. p.54

prior to joining. In this case Pauline had simply followed her father into the movement as she felt it was the 'natural' thing to do. Pauline enjoyed the social aspects of BUF membership and enjoyed life at the women's national headquarters, recounting 'the ceaseless round of activities, the opportunities open to women, and the example set by leading women members of the BUF'.[40] The first women's offices were located at 233 Regent Street, London and paid for by a sympathiser. By January 1934 the Women's Section had moved to 12 Lower Grosvenor Place, London which was also the headquarters for the Youth Section.

A feature of all fascist movements is the cult of leader. Mosley projected himself and the BUF image as a dynamic new force in British politics, a 'modern movement' to distance and contrast the organisation from the conventional 'old' political parties. This had appeal to the young, a sense of moving forward and leaving behind the out-dated politics of the nineteenth century. The emphasis was on action (as their newspaper *Action* was appropriately named), and 'scientific methods' principally the science of eugenics,[41] a fashionable (if not dangerous) idea in Nazi Germany and other parts of the world at the time.

Mosley was the sole and undisputed founder and leader of the BUF. By all accounts he was a brilliant and experienced orator, a tall handsome man with great charm and charisma. This could well have been an attraction for certain women who may have been drawn towards the BUF because they idolised the leader. Both Mosley's future wife Diana and her sister Unity Mitford found Hitler appealing too, seeing him as an embodiment of 'power', a well-known supposed aphrodisiac. This theme of sexual attraction can be further expanded by looking at an account of an ex-member who joined the BUF aged 16, and published in *The Guardian* newspaper in 1978. During the interview the anonymous woman from an East End family of 11 children praises the sexual attraction of male Blackshirts. On seeing a young man dressed in black uniform selling *Action* she recounts:

40 *Ibid.*

41 Eugenics is a social philosophy advocating the improvement of human genetic traits by promoting sexual reproduction for people with 'positive' genes and to discourage reproduction by sterilisation of people with less-desired genes. This is according to those that advocate eugenics such as fascists and Nazis. The doctrine was by no means confined to them. Supporters included members of the left wing intelligentsia such as George Bernard Shaw and HG Wells. Originating in Britain in the 1860s through the work of scientist Francis Galton, eugenic theory became a dominant idea and governmental policy in many countries in the first half of the 20th Century. Its popularity waned particularly after the horrors of the Nazi occupation of Europe were exposed. Today, the science of eugenics is making a comeback due to new genetic science developments.

As he was good-looking, I purchased my first copy of the paper called *Action* much to the dismay of mother's friend [she was Jewish]'.[42] After reading the paper she decided to join the BUF but had to keep it a secret from her parents, her father was a strong Labour man. '[He] would have given me a good hiding.[43]

The woman goes on to explain why she enjoyed belonging to the movement:

'I loved going to the meetings – for a start the boys were good-looking, and plenty to choose from… the feeling of doing something that was secret to everyone in my family'. Eventually she met 'the most handsome boy [she] had ever seen and he came from Bethnal Green'.[44]

She was of course a typical rebellious teenager with a school girl crush for a boyfriend to carry her off to a more exciting place than the East End. She proclaimed that this was the most exciting time of her life. Mosley was her hero and her account of his Albert Hall speech testifies to the extent of her rapture:

We all heard our hero Oswald Mosley speak…it was very thrilling to be part of a crowd 100% behind him. I believe at that time I would have laid down my life for him.[45]

It would appear that this woman was not particularly interested in the ideology of the BUF and seemed to have little or no interest in the political consequences if the movement had come to power.

Another member, known only as Mrs. B., joined the Moss Side Branch in Manchester in 1934. Mrs B. lived next door to the BUF Manchester headquarters where she observed that she was 'attracted to the smartness of the men in their uniforms'.[46] Mrs B. became a Section Leader of the Moss Side women's section and her fiancé was also a member. It is interesting to note here that after their marriage Mrs B. was no longer actively involved in the party, although she remained a member until 1940. We can suspect here that Mrs B. was following the traditional role of a married woman at the time – that of housewife and mother.

42 The Guardian, 4 March 1978 p 11
43 *Ibid.*
44 *Ibid.*
45 *Ibid.*
46 Lunn K. & Thurlow R. (eds.)., 1980. *British Fascism*, Croom Helm, London, p.115

At the age of 18 Yolanda McShane joined the BUF in 1935 along with her mother. Yolanda worked as a women's organiser for the Merseyside Branch in 1936, having previously worked in an East End of London mission. She claims to have worked for the benefit of children, stating in her autobiography that she had given all her pocket money as a child to a charity to enable poor children to have holidays. McShane saw her role in the BUF as one of charity worker to improve living conditions in the East End of London through political ambition:

> I found Mosley's ideas attractive – they seemed to offer a better life for the very poor…Joining the Blackshirts seemed to bring nearer the day when all children would have enough to eat, and also to be able to enjoy the country and the sea that I loved so much myself.[47]

Some BUF branches held parties for local children in need as well as special summer camps and it is probable that McShane's organised such events. She also made speeches on street corners, condemning the "Jewish monopoly of British money and business…Mosley was not racist; he was anti-Jew…it did not seem to me very important, compared with his promise of 'Equal opportunity for all'".

McShane was however, to turn hostile to the BUF as is shown in the extract below, written later, where she describes her growing unease of Hitler and fascism. "His atrocities against the countries he occupied and against the Jews had sickened me…I realised too that in joining the Blackshirts I had been totally misled, they were after all linked with Hitler's politics'.[48]

But what of the legacy of the children of the women who were members of the BUF? Although only one former suffragette was interned in the U.K. – Norah Elam who was imprisoned at Holloway on 23 May 1940 – other BUF women were interned and dispatched to Holloway prison on the outbreak of WWII. Women members may have set about destroying any evidence that they were associated with the movement and in fear that they may be separated from their children. Indeed, Diana Mosley was herself arrested on 29 June 1940 (Oswald Mosley had been arrested the previous month). Her son writes in his biography about the life and politics of his parents, *Beyond the Pale*:

> A gang of police came to Savehay Farm; she was given the choice of either taking or not taking with her eleven-week-old Max whom she was still breast feeding. She was told she would not in any case be able

---

47 *The Star* newspaper, McShane Yolanda. *Daughter of Evil.* 1980 pp.30-33
48 *Ibid.*

to take with her one-and-a-half-year-old Alexander, so she decided not to separate the children but to leave them with their Nanny…On her way to Holloway Diana asked to be allowed to stop at a chemist…to buy a breast pump to get rid of the milk that should have been for her baby.[49]

MI5 documents released in 2002 described Lady Mosley, 'reported on the 'best authority', that of her family and intimate circle, to be a public danger at the present time. Is said to be far more clever and more dangerous than her husband and will stick at nothing to achieve her ambitions. She is wildly ambitious'.[50] The *Daily Telegraph* reported upon the death of Lady Mosley that a diamond swastika was among her jewels.[51]

In 'Children of Blackshirt women live with shame: Mother was a Blackshirt',[52] a *BBC Radio 4* production, James Maw explains that children of Blackshirt women often feel that they have to live with a burden of guilt and shame caused by their mother's fascist sympathies. In a frank autobiographical account, Maw recalls that when he was 11 his mother told him about the Blackshirt meetings she attended in Kennington, London. His mother recounts how she worked in an ink factory as a young girl, and how she hated it: "it was horrible…There I met Primrose…she invited me home. I met her family and fell for it – they were trying to get me to be a Blackshirt". Maw believes that women like his mother were not interested in politics, but rather the comradeship and the smart uniform. As Mosley had proclaimed his movement was to be one like a church, a social club, where ordinary members mixed with well to do women. Maws interviewed Diana Bailey, a daughter of parents who were BUF members who lived in Bognor Regis. At the age of nine she remembers her mother and father in their Blackshirt uniforms, and as children: "We were told to paint slogans on the walls with 'Awake Britain' and 'Perish the Jews'.

Women Membership Numbers

A common theme of articles published in *The Blackshirt* misleadingly claimed that the BUF was the only political party in Britain at the time that boasted its own association for women members. It is true that women in the BUF were working as both officers and rank-and-file members, but, always in co-

49 Mosley N. Op. Cit. p.166
50 BBC News Online (Published: 2003/08/13) *"Oswald Mosley's widow dies."* www.news.bbc.co.uk
51 *The Daily Telegraph 13th August, 2003.*
52 Maws J., 2010. *Children of Blackshirt women live with shame: Mother was a Blackshirt.* BBC Radio 4. 3 Jan., www.news.bbc.co.uk

BUF 'Peace Rally' at Earls Court, London. 16 July 1939. 30,000 people attended. 60 Women's Drum Corps marched Mosley into the hall. Mosley spoke without notes for over an hour.

operation, and dominated by their leader and the male faction of the party. Women were subjugated by male values of the time imitating Mussolini's fascist doctrine – a distinctive masculine set of rules. Nowhere does the party ever mention that these women were on equal terms with the men at committee level, there is nothing to be found in the literature to support this. Under the intended fascist corporate state BUF high command proposed that the women's Domestic Corporation would always be under represented in parliament.

Following the violent events at the BUF Olympia rally in London in June 1934 the Labour Party wanted to know how best to organise itself against fascist expansion in Britain. Consequently the Labour Party instigated a survey named the 'Questionnaire on Local Fascist Activities' and distributed the survey among its 900 divisional groups and affiliated organisations. Within the questionnaire were two questions on women and youth support. Labour Party officials returning the questionnaires reported the existence of fascist women members in at least 55 districts nationwide.

The BUF did not publish their membership numbers, let alone the percentage of women members. However, Mosley did boast during an interview with *Berliner Lokal-Anzeiger* in November 1936 that party membership stood at half a million members, with 500 branches.[53] Labour Party officials put the

53 Gottlieb J.V. Op. Cit., p.45

total number of BUF members in Bristol City at approximately 500, which included an undisclosed number of women. The reply for Bristol East showed no figure for total membership, however the respondent does state that the district did have a women's section.

Special Branch seized BUF party files, which would have included names, dates and addresses, during police raids on the head office, various branch offices and BUF members' homes under the Defence Regulation 18B, beginning in May 1940, but unfortunately these files were eventually destroyed. Therefore, an exact gender ratio of men/women members at any one time is hard to determine. Also, Home Office files did not break membership numbers down according to gender. However, Thurlow, in his academic accounts, believes that women may have accounted for over 20 per cent of the membership.[54] Overall membership numbers varied during the years 1934 to 1939 as the movement's popularity fluctuated, both nationally and at a regional level. Generally these are the accepted figures:[55]

February 1934	17,000
July 1934	50,000
October 1935	5,000
March 1936	10,000
November 1936	15,500
December 1938	16,500
September 1939	22,500

Membership fell in 1935 following violent riots that occurred at the infamous rally held on 7th June at Olympia, London in 1934. Due to the violence perpetrated by the fascists, former fascist supporter Lord Rothermere, proprietor of the *Daily Mail*, withdrew his support overnight. Previous to this the *Daily Mail* was front paging fascist populist propaganda that had driven Mosley's upsurge of political respectability.

Thurlow rightly points out that the papers released by the National Archive (formerly the Public Record Office) pertain mainly to the problems of public order due to the violence that occurred at BUF meetings and identify possible BUF Fascist security guards, some of which were women. Special Branch and government were also concerned about the possibility of fascism getting a hold over mainstream British politics and attempted to gather data about the possible effects of the BUF on British society.

54 Thurlow R., 1987. *Fascism in Britain. A History. 1918-1985.* Oxford: Basil Blackwell
55 Webber G., 1984. Patterns of membership and support for the BUF. *Journal of Contemporary History.* Vol.19, pp.575-606

The figures below are estimates, of attendances at BUF meetings, recorded by Special Branch, and were collected via undercover surveillance at BUF meetings. A small selection of these records survives and act as evidence to the high membership levels of women activists who attended meetings:[56]

Date	District	Men	Women	Women (%)
September 1934	London	3000	450	(13%)
March 1935	London	500	160	(23%)
May 1936	Victoria Park	1120	180	(14%)
June 1936	London	1400	260	(16%)
May 1937	London	800	250	(24%)
July 1937	Trafalgar Square	1900	360	(16%)
October 1937	Brixton	2770	630	(19%)

These figures suggest that on average 17 per cent of the people who attended the above fascist meetings were women.

In other parts of the country such as Dorset West, South and North, surviving records provide us with further evidence of the extent of female membership. Robert Saunders was the BUF District Leader for the county. Anticipating arrest under DR 18B in 1940, Saunders hid the Dorset membership lists inside an encyclopaedia to protect the membership from the authorities. During the expected police raid the police failed to find the list when they searched Saunders' home in 1940. In 1939 total members were listed at being just 59 persons, of which fifteen women were members (25 per cent). Of these fifteen women five had husbands who were also members, four were married women who joined alone and six were single. In May 1938 Mrs Gladys Stephenson became the first Women's Dorset District Leader. Up until this time the Women's Section had to be run from Wessex, suggesting the Dorset region lacked sufficient women numbers.[57]

The role and status of women in the BUF might be presumed to be predetermined by the percentage of their membership. But women in the BUF were organised separately from the men having their own role to play within the party and were kept within the confines of the specially formed Women's Section. The woman's role was to be that of an auxiliary force. The official

56 Gottlieb J.V. Op. Cit., p.47
57 Robert Saunders' Membership List, 30 October 1939, *Saunders Collection* Sheffield University, File E.1. Cited in Gottlieb J.V. Op.Cit., p.82

dictionary definition of the word 'auxiliary' being: providing (additional) help or support, especially with lower rank or of less importance.[58] However, although the Women's Section certainly carried out traditional female roles such as secretarial support, tea making and cleaning the women were also allowed to work in the public sphere. They canvassed for the party, sold Fascist papers and propaganda on street corners and even acted as stewards (bouncers) at meetings. Selected women were also taught the art of speech making, first aid along with self-defence in the form of jujitsu, which interestingly the suffragettes had also used this type of defence training to protect themselves from police brutality. This was illustrated in *The Blackshirt* under the title 'Women Blackshirts – Helping to Build a Greater Britain'.

Fascinatingly Special Branch did collect data on the number of women stewards at BUF meetings, probably because of the para-military style of the movement. The table below shows that at almost every rally approximately 25 percent of the stewards were in fact women members.[59]

Date	Where	Male	Female
25 April 1935	Albert Hall	1500	500 (25%)
24 July 1935	West Ham Town Hall	180	20 (10%)
26 October 1935	Porchester Hall	70	30 (30%)
6 March 1936	Harlsden	12	4 (25%)
16 June 1939	Earl's Court	3000	1100 (27%)

Information about the activities of lesser known women was not recorded. The interviews with four women members by Cullen (1996), represents a very rare example of primary source research undertaken to discover the activities and motives of former women members.

The jobs which these women recorded as having undertaken confirm that the men and women were organised into separate hierarchies, but with women able to perform all the roles undertaken by men. One of the women states that as well as doing secretarial work she also became a trained steward at BUF meetings:

A great friend of mine was in charge of the women's tough squad. We wore slightly different Blackshirts with collars like Mosley's [A fencing style shirt], and were trained to deal with a certain amount of

58 Longman Dictionary of Contemporary English, Longman. 1991
59 Gottlieb J.V. Op. Cit., p.46

violence…I can remember my friend having a pretty tough fight with a communist at the Manchester Free Trade Hall. Fortunately she wore black underwear so managed to come out of it with dignity even when her shirt was ripped off.[60]

These women felt a great sense of commitment to the fascist cause, the movement offering them a feeling of excitement and of belonging that was to encompass much of their time and life-style. Two of the women interviewed by Cullen found love and marriage in the BUF with one of them marrying the District Leader for Birmingham, she stated:

at this time it [the BUF] did become our whole life virtually. We were out weekends and evenings, all our spare time was really devoted to what we believed in.

It is common of course for people to meet future partners in any organisation where people with the same values and beliefs congregate. A social structure was therefore formed within the BUF over the years which united the membership and, of course, sexual bonds took place. Cullen noted that the four women he interviewed all came from families where the parents were conservative voters and of the lower middle classes. One of the women confessed that she had 'no political base at all', and that she simply enjoyed the social aspect of membership; this is common to all political parties. The women's national headquarters offered the women many activities, in fact the BUF took on the role of family. Caution is required when considering the value of primary sources with regard to the women's membership of the BUF. It must be remembered that the recollections of former women members may have been affected by dislocation of memory over the years. In addition these women would have been influenced by the events of 1939 and their personal experiences of internment, not to mention the revelations about the horrors of the holocaust. However, primary source research is of the utmost value especially given the limited resources when investigating the history of the BUF.

Pro-Fascist Suffragettes

Why is it that some women, some former suffragettes, who considered themselves to be feminists, who fought for equal rights for women, were attracted to the BUF - a party that believed that men were superior to women? These were women who were both articulate and well educated, and therefore

60 Cullen S. Op. Cit., p.57

must have comprehended the repressed reality of life for women in Fascist Italy and under National Socialism in Germany. Perhaps they believed that the price for women, to lose their embryonic fight for equality, was a price worth paying to accomplish a fascist dictatorship in power in Britain for the greater good.

Women have an historical stake in fascism. The original Fascist Party in Britain was named the British Fascisti and was interestingly founded by a woman named Rotha Lintorn-Orman, in 1923 and financed by her mother giving £50,000 over to her daughter. Lintorn-Orman was opposed to all women and only some men having the vote and it is generally accepted that she did not engage with the suffrage movement although the police believe she was a former suffragette. Interestingly Lintorn-Orman was once believed by some to have been the lesbian lover of Mary Sophia Allen, yet other research suggests that she married her security guard in secret and they had a daughter named Olive.

The earlier British Fascisti did not wear a uniform but members did carry black handkerchiefs and wore badges on which the initial 'F' encircled the words 'For King and Country'. Members saluted during the playing of the national anthem by flinging their right hand across their chest and touching their badge. By all accounts Lintorn-Orman was a wealthy eccentric heiress and a forthright spinster with a taste for mannish clothes. (She was rather similar in nature to another former suffragette and BUF member, Mary Allen). Lintorn-Orman's mission, as she saw it, was to fight against the evils of Bolshevism and to 'eliminate the evils of universal suffrage', the idea apparently having come to her one afternoon whilst digging in her garden on her dairy farm in Somerset.

Lintorn-Orman came from an army family; her grandfather had been a Field Marshal and army discipline seems to have rubbed off on her. According to fascist reports during WWI she won the Croix de Charite for gallantry whilst driving an ambulance in Serbia. She was not particularly interested in ideology and had little regard for the value of the vote. She urged women to buy only British goods as a means of eradicating socialism. Scandal was a theme which kept recurring in Lintorn-Orman's life, it was alleged by the secret service that 'drunken orgies and undesirable practices took place at her London home'[61]

Lintorn-Orman led the British Fascisti in classic fascist dictatorial style synonymous with fascist authoritarian leadership. The British Fascisti made wild claims about party membership numbers, claiming that at one stage they had 400,000 members. *The Daily Express* however, estimated that membership in reality only stood at a few thousand.[62] Membership numbers were pushed even further downwards by the Home Office, who in 1934 recorded that

61 PRO HO 45/25386/37-40. Cited in Thurlow R. 1988. *Fascism in Britain*. p.56
62 *The Daily Express*, 26 April, 1933, p.3

Rotha Lintorn-Orman.

membership only ever reached 300.[63] The British Fascisti was to merge, against Lintorn-Orman's wishes, with Mosley's New Party in 1931. Lintorn-Orman died on March 1935 on Las Palmas, Canary Islands aged just 40 years from alcohol and drug-related problems.

The BUF was unusual as a fascist movement in that it proclaimed itself to be pacifist and ran numerous peace campaigns. This in itself may have appealed to certain women. The influence of Anna Brock Griggs was considerable. She worked as the BUF's Woman's Propaganda Officer, was in charge of organising the women's camps, and was eager to attract other women by stating the BUF had no desire to go to war with Germany for a second time. Brock Griggs, a former Labour prospective parliamentary candidate, was certainly aware that enfranchisement did not mark the end of women's political activity, since women were politically active both before and after the early 1930s. Can it be supposed then that women were willing to do the spade-work for a party whose elite they had little hope of joining?

Similarities can be found between one arm of the suffragette movement and fascism. Part of the suffragette movement was certainly militant, with women committing crimes such as window smashing and burning government buildings and churches. This militancy was to cause a split both within the organisation and the Pankhurst family. Given this fact, might not a para-military organisation such as the BUF be an attractive option for some members after the fragmentation of the suffragette movement following WWI? As cited earlier, Norah Elam wrote in *Fascist Quarterly* about the similarity between the former suffragette movement and fascism. She states that the women's movement was organised under a single leader with strict discipline, adding that supporters of the BUF (like those of the suffragette movement) came from all classes. This is certainly partly true. Parallels can also be made in so much as women from both movements faced ridicule and hostility on the streets as they

63 Benewick R., 1972. *The Fascist Movement in Britain*. Penguin Press, London. p.31

sold their respective newspapers to promote their propaganda. Verbal abuse was common and the women from both movements experienced being spat upon, name calling and worse. However, Elam drew the incorrect conclusion that fascism was: 'the logical, if much grander, conception of the momentous issue, raised by the militant women of a generation ago'.[64] Elam was, however, correct in her conclusion that both movements were attacked and maligned by the government of the day.

McNeil points out that the 'WSPU had begun as a movement to include working women [working class] in their struggle for the vote'.[65] However, by 1913 the movement had become one in which 'the ladies were respectable and fashionable, with narrow aims, an autocratic structure, an over bearing middle class composition, which led to the estrangement of many of its earlier core supporters', even members of the Pankhurst family. After 1915 the WSPU became more right wing with a nationalist hard-core campaigning for the war effort including speaking and encouraging a national conscription for women to take up war work. Also, *The Suffragette* newspaper was re-named *Britannia* and promoted the internment of any person of 'enemy race' (German) found in Britain. The pro-war element of Christabel Pankhurst's leadership of the WSPU at the outset of WWI was largely based on the realisation that the Kaiser was opposed to women's rights. Millman writes that the message of the WSPU was clear – a victory for Germany would be a disastrous defeat for women's rights. 'A woman's deepest instincts and her reason tell her that Prussia stand for all that is deadly to woman spirit in the world. We will not be Prussianised!'[66]

The WSPU were the militant faction for female enfranchisement and their mantra can be described as being the rhetoric of civil war during a time of social decline. The WSPU was always a small organisation with only 2,000 members at its peak. On the other hand the democratically run National Union of Women's Suffrage Societies (NUWSS), had over 100,000 members and many of its former members went on to join the Labour and Liberal parties. Could it be that the WSPU, under the leadership of Emmeline Pankhurst, was always an authoritarian organisation and which therefore attracted authoritarian personalities? The violent women of the militant movement for a short time occupied the same space as men would traditionally; they demanded equality and used behaviours previously attributed to masculine identification, being honour, war, duty, and respect of leader, during their campaigns. Indeed, was the Women's Social and Political Union a fascist organisation run by a

64 *The Blackshirt,* 2 Nov., 1934. p.8

65 McNeil S. *Votes For Ladies. The Suffragette Movement 1867-1918*. Bristol Radical Pamphleteer. Pamphlet #15. 2nd Ed. 2014

66 Millman, Brock, 2000. *Managing Domestic Dissent in First World War Britain.* Frank Cass

female dictator? Probably not to this totalitarian extreme, but the movement did radicalise women and appealed to women who wanted to take on the establishment and be led by a single leader who displayed characteristics of intolerance towards those that opposed her policies. Many of the WSPU former leading lights became right-wing conservatives, or went on to the join the British Union of Fascists or other fascist organisations. In contrast Sylvia Pankhurst went to the other extreme. Denounced by the Russian revolutionary Lenin for being too left-wing,[67] but going on to help establish the Communist Party of Britain from which she was soon expelled for being too radical. Previous to this she had already broken away from the WSPU, founding, in 1913, the East London Federation of Suffragettes (ELFS) a branch dedicated to supporting votes for the working class which was to be run in a far more democratic way than the WSPU.

In the 1930s, articles regularly appeared in the Women's Section of the BUF press praising the ideology of the Corporate State. Women's disillusionment with the parliamentary democratic process was to be exploited and used to entice women membership using the principle founded by Mussolini, the Corporate State. Mosley promised the creation of a Corporation for married women which would be a means of representation in parliament instead of a traditional elected member of parliament chosen by the constituency to represent both women and men. Propaganda was directed to rubbish the victory of women obtaining the vote with the hope of fuelling female disillusionment with the slow progress of women's rights through representation in parliament and with the democratic system as a whole.

After gaining the vote feminists were indeed suffering from a sense of disillusionment due to the reality that so few women had been elected to parliament. The BUF was quick to capitalise on this in their propaganda. Ex-suffragettes who chose to join the BUF may therefore have been attracted to the movement as a means of entering parliament as BUF candidates. For instance, former suffragette Mary Richardson, who had stood unsuccessfully on three occasions as a Labour parliamentary candidate, went on to be selected as a BUF prospective parliamentary candidate (PPC) for the proposed 1939 general election.

Other former suffragettes with high political ambition were: Norah Elam, standing as the PPC for Northampton; Mercedes Barrington, the PPC for West Fulham and, Mary Allen, pioneer of the volunteer women's police force and commandant of the Women's Auxiliary Service.

When Mosley introduced Norah Elam to her prospective constituents in 1936 he declared that her candidacy:

67 Lenin, V.I, 'Left-Wing' Communism: An Infantile Disorder (1920)

killed for all time the suggestion that National Socialism proposed putting British women back into the home…[she] had fought in the past for women's suffrage. She had been imprisoned, and was a great example of the emancipation of the women of Britain.[68]

Norah Elam, formerly known as Mrs Dacre-Fox, was a leading suffragette in the WSPU and was imprisoned for militant actions three times, on one occasion with Emmeline Pankhurst. Elam was a staunch nationalist working during WWI as a recruiter for the military in South Wales as well as working in a munitions factory. After standing and losing as an independent candidate for Richmond Surrey, and then joining the Conservative Party for a short time, she went on the join the BUF in 1934 along with her husband, Dudley Elam, who was chairman of Chichester Conservatives. She was to prove a high flyer for the BUF and stood in 1936 as PPC for Northampton after becoming BUF County Women's office for West Sussex. Her husband worked as an unpaid receptionist at BUF Headquarters. She was also a prolific writer for the BUF press and was to take charge of BUF finances at the time of the declaration of war in 1939, being so highly trusted by Mosley.

Previously, when Elam was General Secretary of the WSPU she believed that all German nationals should be returned to Germany before the outset of WWI. She started a campaign 'The German Peril'. *The Times* published a quote of Elam's view point in 1918:

We had to make a clean sweep of all persons of German blood, without distinction of sex, birthplace, or nationality…Any person in this country, no matter who he was or what his position, who was suspected of protecting German influence should be tried as a traitor, and, if necessary, shot.[69]

This is extremely ironic considering that she herself was to become a Nazi sympathiser and actively worked to promote their policies on the fascist stage during 1930s Britain. Elam was to argue in *Action*, writing as a 'prominent suffragette leader', that democracy had rendered the efforts for women's suffrage meaningless. From the moment women gained the vote, she claimed, they had, with few exceptions, aligned themselves with the very parties that 'had treated them with such unprecedented contempt'.[70] Here she is associating

68 *Action* No. 41. 28 Nov. 1936. As cited in Gottlieb, 2003. p.64
69 *The Times,* 1918. Quote by Nora Elam. Cited in www.Hollowaylife.net Centre for Business, Arts and Technology, 2014
70 Durham M., 1998. *Women and Fascism*, Routledge p.45

herself with the militant fight of the WSPU, and claiming that the revolution for the women's movement was by no means complete. It was believed she was a Nazi collaborator and on 18th December 1939 her flat was raided by the police. Further raids took place at her office in August 1940, and following this she was interned along with her husband under DR 18B on May 23rd, 1940. She never made an appeal against detention as many other BUF members who were detained were to do, including her husband. After the war Elam attended the famous 18B Social Dance held at the Royal Hotel in London on 1st December 1945, attended by fellow fascist friends who were interned and other supporters of Mosley. Norah Elam was the only former suffragette to be interned being presumed by Special Branch to be in Mosley's secret inner circle and a confidant to his possible collaboration plans with Germany. Mosley always disputed this fact, and claimed under questioning by the police, that he simply handed over his papers to Elam as he feared the BUF headquarters would be bombed in the war or he might be murdered by an angry mob.

Although the movement played on the rhetoric of equality for women as a means of attracting women members, it was in fact 'profound[ly] anti-feminist'.[71] To be a fascist feminist is a contradiction in terms, but the BUF supported the concept of the feminine fascist - an entirely different pedigree of woman. This was to have appeal for some former feminists including those who were leading suffragettes, drawn towards the rhetoric of Mosley's fascism. There were splits within the movement regarding the role of women, both within the body of the party hierarchy and within grass-roots membership. This debate was kept open by ex-suffragettes who had joined the BUF and who then unsurprisingly found they were struggling against patriarchal intellectuals such as Alexander Raven Thomson, the BUF Propaganda Officer.

Pugh, argues that these former suffragette women were in no way misguided or manipulated into joining the BUF, they were middle class and upper class women from Conservative backgrounds, who reacted against conventional politics and became disillusioned for the same reasons as men.[72]

Fascist Roots in the South West of England

The earliest recorded public meeting in the south west was held on the October 18th 1924 in Cheltenham. The *Gloucestershire Echo* newspaper ran with the column headline 'British Fascists. Enthusiastic Cheltenham Meeting.' The paper reported a crowded, energetic, enthusiastic gathering at a meeting held

71 Lewis D.S., 1987. *Illusions of Grandeur: Mosley, Fascism and British Society, 1931-1981.* Manchester University Press, p.53
72 Pugh M., The Women's Movement. *History Review.* Issue. 27. March 1997

at the United Services Hall in Cheltenham. The reporters noted that many ex-servicemen and people from all classes were in attendance to hear about the merits of the anti-communistic and anti-Semitic agenda of the British Fascisti Party, founded by Rotha Lintorn-Orman in May 1923 and financed by her mother. The platform was led by senior military officers and Lady Ismay, the head of the Gloucestershire Women's Unit. During the speeches that were made the party claimed to have 299 members in Cheltenham, with "one lady recruiting officer having 'roped in' 60 members."[73]

The speeches on that evening clearly reflect fascist ideology: fear of a communist revolution spreading from Russia with the on-set of the General Strike; to unite all classes; and to blame the nation's ills on Jews ("a pack of German Jews") and communists:

> …to prevent a Communistic rebellion in our country. The British people in general did not understand the seriousness of the menace, and they know that the British workman, was all right at home, and not by nature a revolutionary. But the communists were working their way towards a revolution by means of a general strike which would mean in a short time misery and starvation to convert into a revolutionary the workman who saw his wife and children in want…The Communist movement was organised by Continental agitators, who were endeavouring to capture the trade unions for revolution and the object of the British Fascists was to get sufficient men and women enlisted to put a stop to the menace of the howling devils

The speaker continued with the usual irrational fear of immigrants and a reference to eugenics ranting:

> …danger of the ever-growing stream of aliens flowing into our cities. Whilst 200,000 British leave this country every year 300,000 aliens flock in overcrowding the cities and 'water down the blood of the country with dirty water'. One of the first things the Fascists would do was to stop this rot (much applause).[74]

After the formation of the BUF in 1932 many local groups in the South West region were formed and these groups were very active, particularly in Bristol and Cheltenham.

73 *Echo*, (*Gloucestershire*) Oct.18, p.4, 1924
74 *Ibid*.

Bristolian poet Mr Ray Webber kindly agreed to share his political memories of 1930s Bristol to enhance the research about BUF involvement in Bristol's political landscape. Mr Webber was born in 1923 into a political family. His father was Leader of the Bristol Communist Party and by the late 1930s. Mr Webber was a member of the Young Communist League. Mr Webber remembers, some years before the beginning of WWII, his father saying to the family on hearing Hitler speaking on the radio, "This means war". On the declaration of war in 1939 "My father burnt all the Communist Party member lists, names, as he believed we would be the first for it when they [Nazis] invaded".

Between 1939 and 1941, until Mr Webber was called up, he worked co-incidentally for fascist "masters" as "they paid the highest wages" at Henbury, Bristol. John Mountjoy, was the proprietor of the Henbury Hill Quarries, Bristol and was an active BUF propaganda official. The site manager, Charles Hewitt managed the running of the day to day dealings in the quarry. Both men had stood as BUF prospective parliamentary candidates for Frome and Bristol South respectively. Mr Webber described Hewitt, who had a gallantry medal for service in WWI walking with a limp and using a stick, "he was respected by the workers". Apparently Hewitt was very kind to his workers, paid the highest wages in the region for manual labour, and gave out medicines to the men for their families for free. Hewitt and Mountjoy were both to be interned during the war under DR 18B, but "Hewitt [and possibly Mountjoy] was released early as he had the knowledge to provide the government with much needed limestone gravel required to urgently build airfields". "Hewitt was released on condition that he was never to discuss anything political". "After I was called up in 1941 to Victoria Barracks, Bodmin, Cornwall, Hewitt sent me a letter which contained a £5 note, saying that he appreciated my work" and that "he knew wages were low in the army". Mr Webber also told of a van in a lock up shed in the grounds of Mountjoy's house that he was once shown by Hewitt. The van had been converted into a mobile speaker's platform which would tour the streets of Bristol during the parliamentary campaigns. "It had 'Vote BUF', or 'Vote Fascist' painted along the side of it".

Mr Webber attended around four BUF meetings in Bristol as a young communist: "not many women at these meetings but this was normal for all the political meetings at the time". "There used to be BUF and other party meetings held outside on the Downs on Sundays, many people used to go and listen to the Blackshirt speaker, women as well as men, it was very popular". The women who did attend would be "middle class and well-spoken", although he believed the female speakers were not from Bristol. Mr Webber recounted one key meeting he attended in c.1938: "They used to meet at the Kingsley Hall,[75] at 8pm. I will never forget a woman in full regalia, very smart. The women were wearing brown uniforms, knee length skirts and high boots - jack boots. Just like I saw at the cinema about the Nuremburg rallies; I could not believe what I was seeing, the woman was strutting around on the stage and she was very impressed with herself but she was a good speaker, a very good speaker. They were raising funds, gaining members and support". Mr Webber believes that this meeting was to fund General Franco's Falangist fascist groups in Spain. "They were 'Friends of Royalist Spain'. I remember the Spanish Civil War newsreels all the time at the cinema. There was violence at the Victoria Rooms, always men, and would be outside the main entrance and the police would come along and say 'look here lads', and 'break it up'". He remembered seeing Blackshirts on the doors guarding the meetings and keeping the communist agitators outside, 'very impressionable and an incredible sight to see in Bristol' were his main feelings about these events.[76]

Bristol Suffragettes who turned Fascist

The emergence of fascism in the Bristol region is chronicled in the local press. As yet there is no evidence of any surviving literature printed by the West Division held in the regional or National Archive. The rise of organised fascism in Britain was reflected in Bristol with the BUF holding regular high-profile meetings in the City and beyond. Accounts in both national and regional press describe violence and a general fear of violence when the BUF were marching and meeting in Bristol. Regional newspapers such as the *Gloucester Journal*, the *Gloucestershire Echo*, and *The Western Daily Press and Bristol Mirror* began to run dedicated columns to report on the latest outrages due to the violent counter-demonstrations the BUF meetings attracted, mainly from young communists.

But, what of the Bristol women members of the BUF? Although there appears to be no written records left behind, it can be surmised that secret membership lists were hurriedly burnt by the female membership, or worried husbands, on the eve of WWII. After all, ringleaders of the BUF were being rounded up and their houses raided by the police. *The Western Daily Press and Bristol Mirror* (5 June, 1940) reported that two Bristolians had been rounded

75 Kingsley Hall on Old Market St was the headquarters of the Bristol branch of the Independent Labour Party (ILP). According to Mr Webber, the ILP's 'open platform' policy had led them to accept bookings for fascist meetings, something which was widely criticised by left-wing party members in the city.
76 Webber R., *High on Rust,* a collected work of Ray Webber's poetry. Tangent Books, Bristol

up and detained in 1940: Messrs C. H. Hewitt and John M. P. J. Mountjoy, proprietor of the Henbury Hill Quarries.

Two known former high profile suffragettes with connections to Bristol were highly active in the BUF. The primary women of interest here are Mary Sophia Allen and Mary Richardson each for their different reasons, but they had useful tools for the movement to exploit.

Mary Sophia Allen OBE (1878-1964)

During the spring of 1933, Commandant Mary Sophia Allen was present at a BUF air rally in Gloucestershire which was attended by 250 Fascists.[77] It was also reported in *The Sunday Dispatch* (11th June 1934), that Miss Eileen Lyons had organised a 'special' flying club for women only members of the BUF in Gloucestershire.[78] The event was held on 20th May, 1934 at Leighterton, Gloucestershire on an apparently disused airfield.[79]

Allen was a keen pilot and loaned her aircraft freely, along with other fascist members' aircraft, for the event. Her aircraft was originally also for the use by the now disbanded Women's Police Volunteers when she was the organisation's commandant. The air rally did not go unnoticed and such was the alarm that questions were asked in the House of Commons. The concern was that the BUF was enabling its own Air Defence Force.[80] The *Gloucestershire Echo* (14 June 1934) reported on its front page that Labour MP Mr Thorme asked the Home Secretary, Sir John Gilmour if he was concerned. Gilmour replied that: "the Chief Constable of Gloucestershire had said that five aeroplanes were on show and giving instruction only and that no action was needed by his department". Thorme replied: "Does he not recognise that a potential dictator must have a private army at his command or otherwise [to] worm his way into the Army and Navy? The *Cheltenham Chronicle* (10th June, 1934), further reported a statement from BUF Air Commander Neale who proclaimed that between 60 and 70 members went up for flights; "It is eventually hoped to have about 140 men in training". Interestingly at about this same time, a fascist friend of Mosley's and BUF organiser for South London, Geoffrey Dorman wrote about aviation in *The Blackshirt* under the pseudonym 'Blackbird'. Dorman was promoting the need

---

77 Dorril S., Op. Cit., p262
78 *The Sunday Dispatch* 11 June 1934, cited in Gottlieb (2003)
79 Leighterton was a grass field about 23 miles from Bristol, on the east side of the A46 and 7 miles south of Stroud. It was set up as a military airfield by the Australian Flying Corps for training 1918. Used for 'society people' during the inter-war period, including Lord Apsley, whilst visiting local country houses. Source: Bristol & Gloucestershire Gliding Club. Club History. Landmarks 2 – The Pre-war club. Ken Brown, Apr. 2015
80 Dorril S., 2006. *Blackshirt: Sir Oswald Mosley and British Fascism.* Viking

Commander Mary Sophia Allen OBE c.1920's.

for a fascist air force in Britain to be modelled on the strengths of the Italian air force. Dorman previously had written articles in the pro-fascist *Aeroplane* until 1930. Meetings such as the one in Gloucestershire were defended by the BUF as merely an attempt for like-minded people to gather for a social event, and the event was only promoted to BUF members in order to acquaint themselves with aircraft.

It is believed that Allen first met Mosley through Norah Elam at the January Club in April 1932. It is reported that she was wearing her 'dark blue, tight fitting tunic, dark blue breeches, black high-top boots [jack-boots] and a peaked cap'. She spoke at the club, following her visit to Germany, 'to learn the truth of the position of German womanhood', and talked of her audience with Hitler and Goering. Allen was a fervent anti-Semite which was reflected in her earlier writings in her *Policewoman's Review*. Although Allen herself never openly joined the BUF she was a secret member of the party. Indeed Mosley added her to his secret list of members to protect her loyalty from police interrogation.[81]

Mary Sophia Allen was born into wealth in 1878 in Cardiff being one of 10 children, and lived in a house with many nannies, governesses and servants. She then went on to be educated at Princess Helena College, Ealing, London. Her father was Railway Chief Superintendent for the Great Western Railway Company who had banished her from his home in Bristol following her arrest

81 *Ibid.*

as a suffragette in 1909. Allen was sentenced to fourteen days imprisonment in Bristol for breaking windows during Winston Churchill's visit to Bristol. She was a former Branch Leader of the West of England Women's Social and Political Union (WSPU) and went to prison three times enduring force feeding during hunger strikes. On the outbreak of WWI she joined the Women Police Volunteers (WPV), which had two training schools, one located in Bristol and the other in London. Allen was awarded the OBE in 1917 for her services during the war. Allen became WPV Commandant in 1920 following the sudden death of the organisations leader, Margaret Damer Dawson; a wealthy aristocrat, who was Allen's live in lover, and also leaving Allen her considerable estate. After the war she campaigned for the foundation of a permanent women's police force and always wore her blue police uniform. She formed the Women's Police Reserve, later to be named the Women's Auxiliary Service, as a private organisation in 1923 which Allen funded herself. Principally this para-military organisation was set-up to fight the communist threat and to respond to the low morals of some women that Mary Sophia Allen was in judgement over. The Metropolitan Police Commissioner eventually ordered that Allen's women's police force was to be disbanded because she had become an embarrassment to the Met. Pervious to this Allen had been arrested in 1921 for impersonating a police officer.

Allen had political ambitions and stood as a Liberal candidate for St. George, Westminster following her obsession to espouse the importance of the uniformed women police officer. Allen made many visits abroad promoting the need for a women's police force including a trip to Germany, where she met Hitler and Goebbels in 1934, and advised them to create a Nazi women's police force. Her links with the BUF were strong, and although not coming out as a member until 1939 she frequently wrote of her fascist beliefs in various publications including *Action*. Her main argument for a fascist state would appear to be to curtail the growing immorality of women and young girls which she blamed on a depraved Jewish influence; a common theme in Nazi propaganda which attempted to concoct a moral panic among the population. Allen escaped internment during the war years but her movements were restricted under DR 18B(2), meaning that she would remain under surveillance and be denied having a vehicle, telephone and other means of communication with the enemy. The *Cornishman* on 4th July 1940 wrote: 'Commandant Mary Allen is a fascist – quite openly and proudly. Sir Oswald Mosley, her leader, is now safely behind lock and key in Brixton Prison, but Commandant Mary Allen is enjoying the sea breezes at her home on the Cornish coast. The country has been assured that "she has not escaped the notice of the authorities". She wrote of Hitler in her book *Lady in Blue*, 'For two and a half hours I sat absolutely entranced by the Chancellor's charming sister listening to the great Dictator…the hypnotic gestures, his passion, his forceful voice and visionary eyes held me spellbound'. She died at a nursing home in Croydon on 16 December 1964.

Allen provides a classic example of how there exists an authoritarian personality type of obsession and drive that is attracted to the radicalised fringes of politics: firstly with her involvement with militarism in the WSPU, and then to become passionately engaged with the far right.

Mary Richardson, (1882-1961)

Mary Richardson had known Mosley before the founding of the BUF as she was a member of his first and short-lived fascist party, the New Party. Her motives for joining the BUF may have been that this would give her the chance to fight and win a seat in parliament - with any party that would take her. Interestingly the political historian Martin Durham makes the argument that former suffragettes who joined the BUF saw no discrepancy between fighting for women's emancipation and fighting for fascism.

Mary Raleigh Richardson's birth is not documented but she may have been born in 1882/3 in Ontario, Canada. However, Boyce (2013), states that Richardson may have in fact been born in Britain, moved to Canada, and returned to the U.K. when she was sixteen.[82] She was to become a notorious suffragette, joining the WSPU after hearing one of the Pankhurst's speak at the Albert Hall. Richardson was extremely militant, being famously prosecuted in 1914 for slashing the Velasquez Rokeby painting of Venus which hung in the National Gallery, London in protest at the persecution of Emmeline Pankhurst while in prison.

Arson, bombing a railway station and smashing windows at the Home Office in London caused her to be arrested no less than nine times and she received prison sentences of more than three years in total. Richardson underwent the torture of forced feeding on three occasions following her arrests; she claimed the effects of this violence against her body left her in ill health for the rest of her life. She was friends with WSPU Bristol organiser Lillian Dove-Willcox, and stayed at her cottage near Tintern Abbey to aid her recovery following a hunger strike. She had also been with Emily Davidson, the suffragette who famously died after throwing herself under the King's horse at the Royal Derby, and had to flee and hide at the nearby railway station to avoid arrest. Richardson was also the target for attack; she experienced having her clothing torn to shreds, and was slapped and struck with the flat of a sword when she attempted to present a petition to King

82 Boyce L., Op. Cit., p.77

Mary Richardson wearing the WSPU colours c.1914.

George V in Bristol on 4 July, 1913, in front of the Victoria Rooms at the top of Park Street. Although arrested and taken to Bridewell Police Station she was later released without charge on the King's wishes. Richardson was also sent to prison on other occasions, together with Sylvia Pankhurst, when she joined, and operated in, the East End of London breakaway WSPU branch. She was a trained journalist and was also known to be a friend of Mussolini when he was a prominent Italian socialist and journalist. In 1912 Richardson sent Mussolini a telegram of congratulations on his appointment as Editor of the Socialist Party newspaper *Avanti!* Their friendship continued until his death in 1943.

Richardson stood as a PPC no less than four times: for the Labour Party in 1916 and then again in 1922; in 1924 after joining the Independent Labour Party, which was further to the left and had links to the Communist Party, and finally in 1931 she stood once again for Labour in Aldershot. Richardson claimed that she learnt her politics from her time and actions in the WSPU; her suffrage experiences were to be a strong theme in her activism. When she stood for official Labour in 1922, she frequently made speeches about prison reform due to her time spent in the prison system and her experience of being force-fed.

On joining the BUF in 1932 Richardson proclaimed, "and having regard to my previous political experience, I feel certain that women will play a large part in establishing fascism in this country." And, "I was first attracted to the Blackshirts because I saw in them the courage, the action, the loyalty, the gift of service and the ability to serve which I had known in the suffragette movement".

The more aggressive role played out by BUF women may have been due to the influence of Richardson, as suggested by Durham (2006), who was for a time the Women's Organising Secretary. Richardson is an interesting character and must have asserted her feminist views within the BUF. A former member remembers Richardson in an interview in the following way:

The moving spirit of this [women's BUF] was an ex-suffragette of great character. She was a fiery speaker particularly at street corner meetings and used to plaster her hair down with Grip-fix so that it would not blow about on these occasions...She lived in a ground-floor flat in a house in Cheyne Walk, London and was a magnet to us young people.[83]

The violence that occurred at the BUF Olympia mass rally on 7th June, 1934 was compared incorrectly by Richardson to that of Black Friday. The BUF lost thousands of supporters, including the *Daily Mail* and the *Sunday Dispatch*, after eyewitnesses saw the violence unleashed by the Blackshirts on anyone, including women, who intervened to ask a question about the motives of the BUF. By contrast on Friday 18th November in 1910, suffragettes were physically attacked and sexually abused: 'the analogy she made was between the suffragettes and fascists as common victims of hooligan violence'.[84] Richardson also made similar references to victimhood through her resistance to forced-feeding, during her suffragette years.

Although politically ambitious, and despite holding high rank in the movement, being a women's organiser for the BUF, Richardson left the BUF in 1935 because she was disillusioned with fascist policy towards women. Women like Allen and Richardson demonstrate how, even though the fascist movement had a misogynist agenda, opportunistic political leaders could win over some feminist woman. These two very different women, and for different reasons, found a role in the BUF during a time when the traditional political parties of the 1930s were not encouraging female engagement in politics, or just as importantly, not seen to be improving the everyday living conditions for ordinary women.

Conclusion - The perils of perception!

The original aim of the suffrage movement was to involve more women in politics and to secure the right to vote. This aim was very much alive in the 1930s as women between the age of twenty-one and under thirty were only able to vote for the first time in 1929, known as the 'flapper vote'. The BUF was in the market to recruit former suffragettes who were disillusioned with the slow progress of female emancipation and its limited achievements for women.

83 Cullen S., Op. Cit., p.57
84 Kean H. 1998. Some problems of construction and reconstructing a suffragette's life: Mary Richardson, suffragette, socialist and fascist. *Women's History Review*. Vol.7, Issue 4, p.485,

The feminist movement had split into several different organisations during the inter-war years and arguments over the age old dispute of whether a woman's place was in the home or out at work remained high on the social and political agenda. Also, the problem of high male unemployment in Britain continued to be partly blamed on women, who were paid lower wages than men and who were therefore seen as 'robbing' men of their masculine right to work, seen by the BUF as the 'virility' of the male right to work.

Certain feminists were drawn away from women's groups after the franchise was gained for women in 1928; some being drawn into radically polarised political parties. Radical movements, as well as the mainstream parties, recognised that women had their uses within the political sphere now that they could exercise their right to vote. The BUF was no exception. The ever astute Mosley realised the BUF needed women to politicise the home – the internal weapon that could convert members of the household through propaganda within the private sphere:

> By the time women were given the vote, the democratic system was crumbling and falling into decay, and they found that the right to put a cross upon a ballot paper once in five years, was merely a new and worse form of slavery for both men and women.[85]

The above passage, which was apparently written by 'an old suffragette' (possibly Mary Allen) appeared printed in *The Blackshirt* in 1935. The article was in response to the embarrassing episode of the resignation of Mrs. H. Carrington-Wood, a north west London organiser. Carrington-Wood dramatically resigned from the BUF through a letter published in *The Star* newspaper where she wrote:

> The promises made on Fascist platforms and in literature are inadequate to appease the anxiety of the womenfolk, who naturally do not want to risk going back to where they were before the days of the Suffragettes.[86]

Some of the women leaders in the BUF were very masculine in appearance. Mary Allen, for example, always wore her Women's Police Volunteers uniform, part of which consisted of jackboots and a monocle. Her hair was cropped like a man's and she lived with several women in her life. It is possible that the motives of such women were simply to be in a position to dominate other

85 *The Blackshirt,* 2 Feb., p.8, 1935
86 *The Star,* 1935.11 Feb. Cited in Durham M. 'Gender and the British Union of Fascists' p.519

women, and indeed men. We should not however conclude from this that they were acting against the best interests of women by attempting to draw women into an ideology dominated by men. After all, political parties of the day were represented mainly by men. These women, from their writings, did genuinely seem to believe that fascism, under the leadership of Mosley, had more to offer women than the established political systems. Furthermore, many of the BUF's women members were openly anti-Semitic and supported the policy of the economic corporate state, believing that this was the only way for women to be represented on equal terms with men, in an unelected parliament.

In contrast Sylvia Pankhurst was by this time leading from the left, founding the British Section of the Women's World Committee Against War and Fascism (WWCAWF). Carrington-Wood, following her resignation from the BUF, went on to give talks about the dangers of fascism for women to organisations such as the WWCAWF and the left-wing Six Point Group, an organisation that campaigned for better working conditions for women. It is evident that, while some former suffragettes were convinced that only fascism could provide women with social and political equality, others felt equally as strongly that fascism would destroy what women had already gained through the feminist movement in the early twentieth century.

The British Union of Fascists was a radical populist movement that disseminated propaganda to promote a perception of an idealised, organic nation state that would serve the needs of women who were frequently neglected by the government at the time. However, this was the peril of perception – fascism always demotes the ideal of womanhood to be the mother, the carer of the home and without a vote. Gottlieb writes that within the fascist state women could only be fulfilled by their biologically destined roles to increase the birth rate, and must accept this as an honour - that they hold the power of procreation.[87]

Society in the 1930s was very different for women from the society women participate in today. British society in the 1930s was far more conservative than at the present time. It is only since the second wave of feminism in the 1960s and 1970s that woman have been accepted in the work place as professional workers; ostensibly having equal conditions with men and pay, although clearly this is still an on-going fight. Mosley was perceived as promising opportunities for women through the corporate state as a means of gaining recognition in society for the work that they undertook within the home. He promised them a fair deal at work too, but as we have seen in the case of Mrs B., (see women BUF members interviewed by Stephen Cullen in the 1980s above), women leaders

87 Gottlieb J.V. op. cit

resigned from their jobs after marrying. If the BUF had come to power it is probable that women would have been confined to the domestic sphere as was the case in Fascist Italy and Nazi Germany.

Initially the BUF did offer women a chance for political recognition within its existing political framework, allowing them the chance to stand as councillors and parliamentary candidates in elections. Mosley recognised that one of the advantages of female membership was that now they had gained the franchise they could then set about converting husbands and families. The levels of female party membership proved that women were a very real asset to the party organisation. Although they found themselves organised separately from the male hierarchy, women were able to prove their steadfast loyalty to Mosley and his political ambitions by giving his party their vote.

Mosley's movement was never a serious threat to British democracy, or indeed, to the established political parties and stability in Britain. The threat for Britain was to come from the tectonic plates of pan-European fascism that had infected all of Europe. The BUF was an irritant to government and to the Labour party, who had seen some of its members move to the far right. The fascist movement was denied mainstream public support due to the actions of left wing activists who sought at every opportunity to disrupt and orally dismiss Mosley's rhetoric. At most the BUF was viewed as a contentious movement in the eyes of the majority of British people. The party was eventually marginalised and condemned when Britain went to war against the Axis power. The BUF was banned on the 10th of July, 1940 under DR 18b(AA), after being declared a proscribed organisation.

According to Gottlieb[88], records show that at least seventy BUF women members were interned and held without trial in Holloway and also on the Isle of Man at a special camp. A fair proportion of these women were titled women, and nearly all were upper middle class or had aristocratic links and military connections. One such woman, Nellie Driver, who did not consider herself a traitor, wrote whilst in Holloway:

> Within those walls confined at night
> I often heard them cry
> Although my woes were far more light
> My own eyes were not dry,
> It seemed that justice came that way
> And haughtily passed by.[89]

---

88 Gottlieb J.V. op. cit
89 Driver N., *The Ballad of Holloway Gaol*. Cited in Thurlow R. (1998), *Fascism in Britain* p.188

Obtaining the vote was considered 'an empty vessel' by the BUF, who made much of the fact that none of the leading suffragettes had won a seat in Parliament, blaming democracy as 'killing them politically'. Mosley stated that, although there were eleven women Members of Parliament between 1918 and 1928, they had achieved nothing. This however is simply not the case. Lady Astor, Unionist (Tory) MP for Plymouth, working with women Labour Members of Parliament helped to get various Bills through Parliament directly concerned with women's issues that the Suffragettes had pressed for. For example, the Pensions for Widows (Widows', Orphans' and Old Age Contributory Pensions Act, 1929), and partial reform of the unfair divorce laws, (The Matrimonial Causes Act 1923), that put men and women on an equal footing for the first time, and equality for mothers in the guardianship of their children when a marriage broke down. Never once were any of the achievements of women MPs, through the democratic process, ever praised or acknowledged by the fascist press. Neither did the Fascist press urge its female or male readers to lobby their respective Members of Parliament on women's rights, social issues that concerned the family, or, the rights of the child. The anti-fascist feminist Winifred Holtby wrote in an article in 1934 that Mosley had criticised women MPs in his book, *The Greater Britain*, as unrepresentative of 'normal' women.

The BUF was in conflict with the traditional values of feminism. Critical of what the suffragette movement had achieved, the BUF sanctioned a pro-fascist propaganda war aimed at women, employing and exploiting the frustrations of the lack of advancement in society and politics since women had won the right to vote, through promoting former suffragettes who had become members. Failures of the suffragette movement were targeted, especially by emphasising the lack of women who had been able to become members of parliament since gaining the vote. Poverty and bad housing still existed in Britain under democracy and the democratic system was blamed by the BUF to be failing women. This led to Mary Allen stating that "national socialism was their only hope".[90] Many other women members such as Yolande McShane felt passionately that fascism was the only means of achieving a genuinely fairer society. However, some of these same women, in the light of events during the Second World War came to appreciate the true nature of Fascism and Nazism and what their adherents were capable of inflicting upon other nations. These same women ultimately felt that they were misled by the leadership, not only by Oswald Mosley, but also by influential women section leaders of whom they once thought of so highly.

Although the BUF was never a threat to democracy due to low levels of membership, the women who found fascism appealing did so because they

90 Durham M. *Op. Cit.,* p.521

lacked faith in the democratic process. Women became frustrated when politicians failed to meet their needs in society. Those needs were not only issues of political equality but also social issues such as bad housing, high infant mortality, lack of women's rights in the job market, lack of available birth control and low wages. Social and political inadequacies affect the whole of society, men, women and children, but it can be argued that during the inter-war period it was working-class women who bore the brunt of appalling conditions in the home, often within inner city areas such as the East End of London and the industrial cities of the north, regions that the BUF targeted.

The militant actions of the WSPU were a form of political extremism that was overseen in an autocratic manner from the top down. Indeed some argue that the WSPU was a terrorist group increasingly perpetrating acts of violence on civilians, such as fire bombings in crowded areas and the destruction of communications (post-box burning and telegraph wires being cut), which also occurred in Bristol. Cultural violence was another tactic: most famously when Mary Richardson smashed Velázquez's Rokeby Venus in London's National Gallery. Mummy cases were damaged in the British Museum; and bombs discovered in the Royal Theatre in Dublin during a packed lunchtime matinee attended by Prime Minister Asquith.[91]

Left wing feminists were often to fight against the fascist cause. For example, Sylvia Pankhurst openly condemned the BUF and the former suffragettes who had joined the movement. The murder of Italian socialist Giacomo Mattcotti in 1924 by Mussolini had prompted her to form the Women's International Mattcotti Committee who were to campaign for the freedom of Abyssinia, (Ethiopia) after the Italian invasion in October 1935. Sylvia Pankhurst demanded that:

> the Home Secretary should imprison Sir Oswald Mosley along with… Mary Richardson, and another former suffragette, Norah Dacre-Fox for 'incitement to violence". Pankhurst went on to make the point that if she had been sentenced on that charge (incitement to violence) "why should fascists, with their virulent anti-Semitism be exempt?

On the other hand, Emmeline Pankhurst's youngest daughter Adele Pankhurst Walsh had begun her political road to radicalisation at the age of 21 in 1906, when she heckled Churchill and Lloyd George and slapped a policeman. As a consequence she was sent to Strangeways prison in Manchester charged with assault. After being banished to Australia in 1914,

91 Riddell F., 2015. The Weaker Sex? Violence and the Suffragette Movement. *History Today,* Vol. 65, Is.3, Mar.

following her estrangement from her family due to her left wing leanings, (her mother bought her a one way ticket to Melbourne), Adele joined the Victorian Socialist Party. She also flirted with communism, but eventually joined the fascist Australia First movement. Her political path verged sharply from militant activist on the far left and then to the ultra-right, which perhaps gives us an illustration how for some women politics was an ever evolving sprint to find a power base within political organisations that might permit politically motivated women to share political office with men. After all, these were women, who despite winning the vote, were disillusioned with the old gang of politicians.

The former Suffragettes who became fascists believed that fascism under the leadership of Mosley, offered that essential degree of non-conformity in its ideology and had the potential to utilise the hard-won women's vote - to do their leader's bidding, and obtain power though fascist rhetoric. These women were naïve on three points as they failed to see that whilst Mosley and his movement would gladly accept the impact of a significant number of women adding to the vote for his cause, he would exploit their activism and nostalgia for the suffragette days. Firstly, the women misjudged that traditional male values would still dictate what their role in society, and within the party machine, would be. Secondly, that fascism was not going to threaten the conventional democratic process in Britain because membership levels were always low. Thirdly, the events in Europe, the path of National Socialism that led to the formation of the Axis alliance and the declaration of war which in turn led to the closing down and virtual destruction of fascism in Britain was under estimated by the women too. Although these women had valid and understandable reasons to look for a further political cause following the success of the suffragette movement, they had moved too far to the right when joining the British Union of Fascists. Some women serving time in prison, firstly as suffragettes, and then ultimately as fascist collaborators. They had experienced the Perils of Perception!

List of Fascist Detainees from South West England

The British Government introduced Defence Regulation 18B on the outbreak of the Second World War in 1939 and it was subsequently used during the war years. This effectively meant that, for the first time British citizens could be imprisoned without charge if the Home Secretary considered that it was in the national interest during wartime. Arrests occurred mainly during September 1939 and May 1940, although some 18B orders continued to be issued after this date.

The government did not make public a list of BUF detainees but the reported number from the War Cabinet office was put at 753 persons. (CAB 65/10 WM(40)). However, the numbers could have been as high as 1,054 according to releases to date. The original list of those detained under DR 18B during the first wave of arrests was released in May 1997. A Second Issue was then released, replacing the original list, in May 2001 containing newly discovered names. Following the Freedom of Information Act other BUF detainee's names have been discovered since. Although at the time their names were not made public by government a small number of BUF members arrested under DR 18B were reported at the time in the national and local press. According to the Friends of Oswald Mosley (FOM),[92] the detentions were far from consistent with apparently insignificant members being arrested while some important members kept their liberty. Why should this be? As yet we do not know. Perhaps this was a tactic to protect BUF families linked to important officials and to save embarrassment for government, or with connections to high ranking military families, the aristocracy and royal family. This prompts speculation that this may have been a tactic to shield well-connected BUF members. (See Appendix below).

The main internment camp for both men and women BUF members was set up on the Isle of Man following a new Act of Parliament, the Isle of Man (Detention) Act 1941. The men stayed at Peveril Camp, Peel and the women at Rushen Camp, Port Erin. Life at the camps was said to be fairly liberal with freedom of association and entertainments such at trips to the cinemas.[93] Many of the detainees were interrogated by MI5 (British domestic counter-intelligence and security agency), at Latchmere House Remand Centre, Ham Common, Richmond, Surrey in 1940 before being sent elsewhere. Holloway prison was where many women were to be interned, including Dianna Mosley, Norah Elam and Anne Brock Griggs (Chief Women's Organiser of BUF until February 1940). Oswald and Diana Mosley were allowed to reside together in Holloway.

The list below contains names some of the known detainees from the south west region of England. It is suspected that some names are missing, whilst other names on the full list do not state the region where the person was active.

92 The Friends of Oswald Mosley (FOM) formed in 1982. FOM are a far right group who organise dinners and reunions showing film of Mosley's speeches. They can be found at www.oswaldmosley.com
93 *Defence Regulation 18B*. Sourced at www.en.m.wikipedia.org

Name	Region	Remarks
Jack Austin	BUF District Leader East Bristol	Later became a Buddhist monk
Olive Baker	Bath	
Lucy Temple Cotton	Exeter	Mother of Rafe
Rafe Temple Cotton	PPC Exeter	Regional Inspector Devon
Walter A Crowle	Devonport	
Robert Donaldson	St. Austell	
Claude Duvivier	District Leader Exmouth	
Rev. G.H. Dymock	Bristol	Vicar, St. Bedes, Bristol
Vincent Edmonds	Dorset District Treasurer Dorset West	
Jack H. Forward	District Leader Exeter	
Thomas Frank	Bristol	
Charles Gardner	London and Gloucester	
Richard Lionel George	District Leader Gloucester	
Charles H.W. Hewitt	District Leader Bristol	
Frederick George Higham	Cheltenham	
Comdr. Charles E. Hudson	District Leader Bognor Regis	PPC Bognor Regis and Chichester
Alma Violet Hudson	Women's District Leader Bognor Regis	Wife of Charles Hudson
Ralph Gladwyn Jebb	Contract Officer Wiltshire 1935. Regional Inspector Wessex.	Capt. Royal Scots Reg. WWI. PPC Dorset West

Name	Region	Remarks
Constance E. Mitchell	Women's District Leader at times for Frome, Bath, Radstock and North Somerset	
John N.P.I. Mountjoy	District Leader of Bristol Branch	Founder member
Earnest Norman	BUF Team Leader in Bath	
R.J.A Stephens	District Leader Cheltenham	
Dr. H.M. Stephenson	Dorset	M.C. Royal Army Medical Corps, Husband of Gladys, Women's District Leader Dorset West (not detained)
Cecil G. Wimhurst	Asst. District Leader Bognor Regis	
James A Wonfor	District Leader Dorset North	Sgt. 78th Canadian Battalion WWI

The full list can be found at *The Defence Regulation 18B British Union of Detainees* Complied by the Friends of Oswald Mosley (FOM) November 2008: www.oswaldmosley.com

Appendix

In the early 1980s there was a campaign for the Public Record Office (now the National Archive) to open the "Mosley papers", Special Branch and other records that remained closed "for reasons of national security" despite thirty years having passed. Bristol Radical History Group member Di Parkin was the campaign's historian. Lady Diana Mosley supported the campaign to open the records and she attended a public meeting at Poplar Town Hall, London. She told Di Parkin at the meeting that she objected to the fact that she had been imprisoned, whereas other (presumably aristocratic) friends of hers, with the same sympathies had remained free. Lady Mosley wanted their names to be made public. In addition, veterans of the Cable Street battles with Mosley were also present at the meeting and refused to shake Lady Mosley's hand. Some of the papers were subsequently released.

Interview:

Mr. Ray Webber. 2016. Memories of Women Fascists in Bristol. Interviewed by Rosemary Caldicott at Mr. Webber's home on the 18th July 2016.

Further recommended reading:

Boyd N. *From Suffragette to Fascist. The Many Lives of Mary Sophia Allen.* The History Press, 2013

Backwith D. & Ball R. *Bread or Batons? Unemployed Workers Struggles' in 1930s Bristol.* Bristol Radical Pamphleteer. Pamphlet #19. 2012

Kean H. *Some problems of construction and reconstructing a suffragette's life: Mary Richardson, suffragette, socialist and fascist.* Women's History Review. 7:4, 475-493, 1998

McNeil S. *Votes For Ladies. The Suffragette Movement 1867-1918.* Bristol Radical Pamphleteer Pamphlet #15. 2nd Ed. 2014

Notes on British Union of Fascists newspapers:

The Woman Fascist. Newsletter for women fascists, established in March 1934. Short-lived and merged into the *The Blackshirt.* Only one edition is known to have survived. Established to cover 'news and problems peculiar to women members'.

Action. (1936-1940). First published on February 21, 1936. A weekly newspaper that became the official voice of BUF propaganda. Would also include film and book reviews and aimed at recruiting new members and maintaining links with BUF sympathisers. It continued in publication until shortly after the internment of Sir Oswald Mosley on Thursday 23rd May, 1940*

The Blackshirt. First a weekly and then a monthly newspaper covering the period of February 1933 to May 1939. In 1934 also issued a periodical *The Fascist Week*. Following the launch of *Action* the focus of *The Blackshirt* changed and was printed mainly for card-carrying members of the movement.*

The East London Pioneer. Launched in October 1936. Short-lived newspaper distributed in the London Boroughs of Bethnal Green, Bow, Hackney, Shoreditch and Stepney.

Fascist Week. Printed from November 1933 to May 1934. Later incorporated in *The Blackshirt* during 1934.*

*The Fascist Quarterly.*** 1935-1936. A theoretical journal printed by the BUF, edited by Angue Macnab. In 1936 it became the *British Union Quarterly.***

Union. Publication of the Union Movement, a political Party founded in Britain in February 1948 by Oswald Mosley and funded by his wife Diana Mitford after Mosley's death. **

* Source: The National Archive, London
**The University of Sheffield

Some of the above newspapers can be viewed at the University of Birmingham, Cadbury Research Library: Special Collections. The collection was given to Mr Wallder in 1989 by the late Robert Saunders, close colleague of Sir Oswald Mosley and District Leader of the British Union for Dorset West.

Some fascist publications are available where indicated at The University of Sheffield Library: Special Collection, British Union Collection.

Cambridge University Library holds copies of *The Blackshirt.*

Authors Note: Although I have read mention of a western region fascist newsletter I have not been able to source any surviving copies as yet.